ANGUS WILSON

JAY L. HALIO

OLIVER AND BOYD
EDINBURGH AND LONDON

OLIVER AND BOYD LTD
Tweeddale Court
Edinburgh 1

39A Welbeck Street
London W.1

First published 1964

823 WIL
0050014233

Printed in Great Britain for Oliver and Boyd Ltd
by Robert MacLehose and Co. Ltd, Glasgow

CONTENTS

ACKNOWLEDGMENTS

I should like to acknowledge a personal debt to Mr Angus Wilson, who through his agents Curtis Brown Ltd generously made available to me unpublished copies of the television plays "After the Show" and "The Stranger." Apart from encouraging my work from its inception and answering a number of my queries, Mr Wilson read the manuscript of Chapters I and IX and made a number of useful corrections on matters of biographical fact that I had somehow falsely inferred. Professor Hugh G. Dick of the Department of English, University of California, Los Angeles, kindly made available to me the stenographic typescript and the recordings of Wilson's original Ewing Lectures for 1960. For a chance to read the typescript of *The Wild Garden* as I was completing the final version of this book, I am indebted to Mr Robert Zachary and Mr August Frugé of the University of California Press. My friend and colleague Professor Hugh B. Staples read the entire manuscript before editing and offered many helpful comments; thanks to his critical eye the reader has been spared more than a few gaucheries of style and at least one unintended (and therefore doubly ironic) parlaying of Wilson's wit. My thanks are due also to the editors of *Critique* and *Modern Fiction Studies* for permission to draw from material previously published in those journals. To my wife, who bears the dedication, I owe far more than my gratitude for her careful reading of both the final typescript and the proofs.

The photograph on the front cover is reproduced by permission of Giséle Freund.

J.L.H.

FOR
JUNE

ABBREVIATED TITLES
BY WHICH ANGUS WILSON'S WORKS
ARE CITED IN REFERENCES

References are to the English editions of Wilson's books, published by Martin Secker and Warburg.

A.S.A.	=	*Anglo-Saxon Attitudes.*
B.O.M.	=	*A Bit Off the Map.*
H.A.	=	*Hemlock and After.*
E.Z.	=	*Émile Zola: An Introductory Study of his Novels.*
Mrs Eliot	=	*The Middle Age of Mrs Eliot.*
M.B.	=	*The Mulberry Bush.*
O.M.Z.	=	*The Old Men at the Zoo.*
S.D.D.	=	*Such Darling Dodos.*
W.S.	=	*The Wrong Set.*
W.W.	=	*Writers at Work*, The *Paris Review* Interviews, ed. Malcolm Cowley.

CHAPTER I

BIOGRAPHICAL INTRODUCTION

Among the many new writers to blossom into print after the Second World War, Angus Wilson appeared somewhat unexpectedly. He himself had no thought of ever becoming a writer and, as a cataloguer for the British Museum in 1936, he had reason to feel that there were quite enough books already—too many, in fact. Writing began as a hobby, although even his earliest published stories have little of the amateur or dilettante about them. An immediate success, he was later confused by careless critics with several other writers then emerging—the so-called Angry Young Men—to whom he had some superficial resemblance. But when he started publishing, Wilson was already in his middle thirties, having been born on 11 Aug. 1913. This fact alone would account for the wide range of social experience not available to writers like John Wain, a dozen years his junior. Anxieties such as his parents suffered during the First World War, the flamboyant life that many of his older friends and relatives lived in the nineteen-twenties, the first full onslaught of leftist intellectual and political reaction—these are some of the things the "Angry" group could not know, certainly not in the same way. That even Wilson could have felt the impact of all this acutely enough to find it useful as a writer many years later must presuppose an unusually precocious child, but we have his own word for it that, in the ways that matter for a novelist, he was.

He was christened Angus Frank Johnstone-Wilson, the son of William Johnstone-Wilson of Dumfriesshire

and the former Maude Caney of Durban, South Africa.
Since his parents were then both middle aged and had
five other sons (the youngest of them was already
thirteen), we can appreciate the problems of temperament and upbringing that inevitably beset their last
child. He was "a very spoilt, frightened, untruthful
child," as he admits in "Bexhill and After." He was also a
lonely, sensitive, and imaginative boy rather isolated
among adult company; it is no accident that the first
story he wrote, "Raspberry Jam," has just such a boy
as its central character. His father lived on a private
income which, together with his wife's money (in amount
equal to his), left them comfortably well off at the time
of their marriage in 1889. During years of rising costs
and decreasing dividends, however, their income was
less able to meet their needs, especially as Mr Johnstone-
Wilson felt a very strong need to gamble. Indeed, during
Wilson's early childhood the family was frequently on
the verge of poverty, if always a very genteel poverty.

Shortly after the First World War, following one of
these financial crises, the family went to South Africa,
to visit his mother's relatives. "Union Reunion," one of
Wilson's earliest stories, draws upon his recollections of
that visit, and though the plot is fictitious, Harry's
"superior English" attitude towards Laura's family
derives partly from his parents' own marital conflict.
"My father had always brought me up to look down
socially upon my mother's 'colonial' family," Wilson
says; "they worked hard, had no or few interests outside
small commerce, and became rich; he did no work,
played very hard, and lost all the money he had."[1] It is
evident that Wilson's father was a raffish, financially
irresponsible person; by contrast, his mother appears to
have been a more proper, cautious, but brave person
who put up with a very great deal—if not always with a
very good grace. Both parents, indeed all of the family,
were highly emotional and given to histrionics, traits

that, bequeathed to their youngest son, found a most useful outlet in his writing of fiction.

His formal education up to the time of entering Westminster School was, to say the least, irregular. After a series of six or seven kindergartens—his parents were then frequently on the move, a step ahead of their creditors—young Angus went to Seaford, to a preparatory school operated by one of his elder brothers. Up to then, he says, he had received "no serious education whatsoever." At his brother's school, he got an education which, if not altogether conventional, was good. Moreover, it had the important advantage of considerable freedom that, along with the kind of freedom he later enjoyed at Westminster, gave ample scope to his nascent powers of mimicry and invention. These powers were nourished by an assortment of absurd or eccentric masters, visiting dignitaries, and a group of fellow pupils easily led into acting games in which their instigator appropriated to himself all but the most boring roles. Historical romances and the novels of Dickens—the latter a continuing interest—were the chief sources for his private fantasies as for his acting games. But long before leaving his preparatory school, Wilson had become so sophisticated as to relish musical comedies and revues and, in his last year, to set this "sophisticated" tone among the school's prefects.

In 1927 he entered Westminster School as a day boy, living with his parents in London in a small private hotel, one of the many shabby-genteel establishments that housed them during this period. Fearful at first of terrible bullying that might await him at school, Wilson actually experienced none at all. "If life at Westminster had a defect, it was that it was for long periods rather boring, at any rate as I crept up the Classical side. It was an extremely civilized place— tolerant, as unenthusiastic as it was unprejudiced, with a large variety of London boys claiming, I suppose, 'upper-middle-class' backgrounds."[2] Among these boys Wilson found several with whom he made close and lasting friendships. He continued his habits of invention and imitation, but some of his stories were apparently so "peculiar" as occasionally to cause outrage among either his friends or, more understandably, their parents. (Compare, for example, the effect of his story-telling upon Otterhead and Mulready-Grebe—two fictitious school fellows—in "Skeletons and Assegais.") He was known by those outside his circle as "the mad boy" or "the boy with the hair," because of his odd manner, his untidy appearance, and particularly his large shock of yellow, crimped, quite long hair. Despite his appearance, he claims never to have been treated with overt rudeness: this information about the way others saw him was obtained from his friends—"an excellent introduction," he concludes, "to the ways of adult life."

When he was fifteen, his mother died, and Wilson only just got back to the hotel in time. Her death was profoundly disturbing—much more than his father's in 1938 or any of the sudden deaths he later witnessed—for his attachment to her was far deeper than he realised. In ways other than causing conflicts which were to become useful in his writing, the event is momentous because from that time on Wilson was drawn into intimate association with families like the Pickering Walkers (dedicatees of *Such Darling Dodos*) with whom he experienced a different kind of life. His own family were snobbish, materialistic to a large extent, and certainly non-intellectual. While they could and did make important claims upon his affections, they made none upon his mind. These adoptive families, by contrast, were people like Bernard and Ella Sands in *Hemlock and After* or the Padleys in *The Mulberry Bush*, whose social, political, and aesthetic ideas opened up for him new modes of awareness. They were nineteen-thirties liberals, rich but leftist in their ideas and attitudes, who sincerely wished to bring about a good life for everyone—the poor, the handicapped, the persecuted—but who were at the same time cut off from any reality that would either bring their dreams into being or, on the other hand, reveal the practical social and political implications of what they advocated. Virtuous impulse in conflict with irresponsible attitudes and behaviour largely characterised their way of life, and this—for Wilson, at any rate—foreshadowed the "collapse of liberalism" in our time. The theme is of major importance in his fiction and drama, and it remains for him (as he said in his Ewing Lectures) the most moving concern of our age.

Meanwhile, at school, other forces were at work strengthening, illuminating, and tempering the youthful intellectual pretensions of Wilson and his friends. Lytton Strachey, Aldous Huxley, and Evelyn Waugh became favourite reading and were to have important consequences in the satirical mode of Wilson's own writing later on. Of the three, Huxley perhaps deserves particular consideration. He was the first "modern" author to whom Wilson really responded—as opposed to Galsworthy, whose *The Forsyte Saga* advanced the values of his family, against which he was then actively rebelling. But Huxley is also important as a sign of Wilson's development in the nineteen-thirties, at Oxford, when he first felt strongly the adolescent quality of *Antic Hay* and its sequels. As late as 1955, however, he could still mingle praise with criticism of that "brilliant young form master, that sophisticated, witty young uncle who emancipated us from the suet pudding hopelessness of our youth, who could do so because in great degree his own emotions, his own phobias were ours. . . ."[3]

But there were other masters as well. Chief among them were John Edward Bowle, who first interested Wilson in history at the same time that he emphasised in his teaching such values as "modern," "civilised," and "an alpha mind." Through Bowle, Wilson was fed a diet of Spengler, Croce, Roger Fry, Freud, Cole, Gerald Heard, and others—from which he almost died as a result, he says, of mental indigestion.[4] But Bowle was equally responsible for introducing Wilson and his friends to people like Harold Nicolson, Mahatma Gandhi, John Betjeman, and Lord Alfred Douglas. He appears to have been a most perceptive as well as energetic man, and rightly prophesying that Wilson would not get a scholarship to Oxford, urged him to write novels. The effect of Bowle's "enthusiastic" approach to teaching was carefully balanced, however, by the senior history master, Lurie Tanner, the Keeper of the Abbey Muniments. Though equally "civilised," Tanner taught his pupils the virtues of decorum and good sense. Wilson acknowledged his gratitude to both of these masters, and indeed the alternation of such opposite dispositions as theirs appears to form the basis of Wilson's own character and of his wit.

In 1932, on a small income provided by his mother's legacy, Wilson went to Merton College, Oxford, to study medieval history. All efforts to convert him to Christianity before he left Westminster had proved fruitless. He had been raised as a Christian Scientist by his mother, but her influence, too, seems ultimately to have had no greater effect than to prejudice him against most of the traditional forms of religious devotion, especially those most conducive to ostentatious piety or obvious hypocrisy. He was then and remains to-day a pagan, though a Puritan in his paganism. At Oxford, his training in history was largely slanted towards Marxist interpretation. Coupled with his class-conscious up-bringing, this training explains the social preoccupations and overtones of his work. Acting was then his special hobby, and he once thought seriously of making it a career. But having done well in his degree, he was encouraged to change his mind. At the close of his schooling at Westminster, he had read widely and passionately in the novels of Dostoevsky, Turgenev, and Tolstoy, but he seems not yet to have thought seriously of Bowle's suggestion that he become a writer himself. For two years after leaving Oxford, in fact, he took such diversified jobs as secretarial work, tutoring, helping his brother run a restaurant, and acting as a social organiser. These were Depression years, and jobs were hard to come by.

In 1936, he went to the British Museum's Department of Printed Books in a position more commensurate with his academic training and one having, besides, the promise of built-in security and stability. The Depression was not yet over, and Wilson's personal background was characterised by anything but security and stability. During this period, when he worked and lived in London, he engaged in much political activity ostensibly designed to prevent the war everyone felt was coming. But such activity, he now believes, was essentially escapist, busy work that devitalised the threat by constant talk of it. Nevertheless, this association with other liberal-minded intellectuals, whose ideas, like his, reflected their exposure to Freudian psychology and Marxist social theory, helped to form the permanent bent of Wilson's mind.

The War, when it came, brought him to the Foreign Office, where he was employed in affairs that apparently must still be kept secret. But although the exact nature of his work cannot be divulged, he gives a good idea of the conditions of his job in "Christmas Day at the Workhouse." It was an atmosphere unlike anything he had known, and being billeted with a widow and her daughter, whose way of life completely differed from his, did not help his growing sense of isolation. Eventually, he felt that the emotional tensions under which he had spent most of his life were beginning to cause him anxieties he could no longer entirely control. His

favoured techniques of social adjustment, such as
clowning and mimicking, failed to help him among his
new associates. His innate desire to please thus deprived
of its usual satisfactions, his situation became more
complicated when for the first time he fell deeply and
seriously in love. In *The Wild Garden* he speculates that
his father's death a few years earlier (and the conse-
quent release he felt from their over-close, intense
relationship since his mother's passing) may have had
something to do with an affair that now plunged him
into making new demands of himself and others that
could not be gratified. He was at last headed for the
nervous breakdown that in one way or another he had
for years managed to elude. Although suffering from
states of acute anxiety, he did not give up his job, but
continued working sporadically in order to maintain
some hold upon the fragments of his former existence.
The loneliness and despondency he then experienced
became the occasion for more earnest thinking about
himself and the world than his previous intellectual and
political activities—later characterised in his writing as
insidious if understandable modes of self-deception and
evasion—had ever permitted.

At the end of the War, he returned to the British
Museum, where he was first put in charge of replacing
some 300,000 books destroyed in the bombing. Feeling
that his Museum job would be too depressing, and still
suffering from the effects of his breakdown, he began
writing in November 1946. "Writing seemed a good way
of diversifying my time," he recalls. "I was living in the
country and commuting to London then and I could only
do it at week ends. That's why I started with short stories:
this was something I could finish, realize completely in a
weekend."[5] It was not very long before he had a sizeable
collection of stories. He showed some of them to his friend,
Robin Ironside, the well known painter, who in turn asked
to show them to Cyril Connolly, the editor of *Horizon*.

Connolly published two—"Mother's Sense of Fun" (November 1947) and "Crazy Crowd" (April 1948). Another, "Realpolitik," was published in *The Listener* (16 Sep. 1948). A friend at Secker and Warburg, John Pattisson, asked to have a look at the other stories, and owing something also to Frederic Warburg's hunch, *The Wrong Set* was published in 1949. Despite the disappointing sales of other collections of stories in England, the book was very successful both at home and abroad. The next year, a second collection, *Such Darling Dodos*, was published and became a Book Society recommendation.

Wilson's career as a writer was launched. However, he still remained a full-time civil servant, for despite the success of his stories, he could not afford to abandon his job at the Museum until several years later (1955). His many varied contacts there (now as Deputy Superintendent of the Reading Room) are suggested in his lively essay, "The World's Greatest Museum," and certainly they have had the important function of adding to his fertile imagination characters and ideas that could be developed in fiction. For example, a remark overheard in the Museum canteen about the dating of the Sutton Hoo burial ship suggested the theme of professional responsibility in *Anglo-Saxon Attitudes*. Many of the people in that novel, too, derive their characters from Museum personnel, such as Mrs Salad, who owes a good deal to an elderly woman who kept the Ladies' Cloak Room. The writing he did up to then—more stories, reviews, broadcasts—was still done during week ends, until a publisher approached him about doing a critical study of some Continental writer. By a process of elimination, Émile Zola was finally agreed upon as unimportant enough for a relatively unknown writer like Wilson to write about—Proust, Dostoevsky, and others having been pre-empted for the work of more famous authors. This study is significant

for Wilson's development as a novelist because up to
then he had only written short pieces of fiction, and his
research at the Bibliothèque Nationale showed him that
his proposed method of composition was right. In a
sense, from Zola's notebooks Wilson's novels also were
born.

Émile Zola: An Introductory Study appeared in 1952 and,
in the same year, *Hemlock and After*. To write his first
novel, Wilson took a four-weeks leave from the Museum,
but this amount of time does not include the copious
note-taking that was and is essential to the gestation of all
of Wilson's novels. This preliminary work goes on in
the ratio of three books of notes to five notebooks of
actual text and, to a lesser extent, is important also in
the composition of his short stories.[6] Because of this note-
taking, a function he describes in some detail in his
Paris Review interview,[7] Wilson found it easy, especially
at first, to write swiftly once actual composition began.
His novels exist in one draft only, with corrections and
additions (usually very few) inserted later. The chief
exception is his play, *The Mulberry Bush*, the only work he
has ever extensively re-written and the one that was
responsible for his resigning, at the age of forty-two,
from his safe and stable job at the Museum. For once
he was involved in getting a play produced, Wilson
realised that he would be in for hours of conferences and
rehearsals that would no longer permit him to keep his
other full-time job. Nor would a leave of absence again
serve his purposes. But doubtless among such considerations was the recognition that he had at last
arrived at a real turning point in his life. This he faced
with both courage and honesty, committing himself
henceforward entirely to the profession of letters, a
decision he has since had little cause to regret.

Leaving the British Museum afforded Wilson time
not only for more sustained literary efforts, but for other
things as well, some of which have had an indirect but

none the less important bearing on his writing. He was at last free to assuage his life-long hunger for travel, and not only the setting of an early episode in *The Middle Age of Mrs Eliot*, but also one of its major themes derive from his trip to the Orient in 1957. After a day's flight over desert landscapes he overheard someone crying in the Karachi airport cloakroom and began to wonder how he would feel if upon his return home he found that he had lost everything. Although at Bangkok (his destination before Tokyo) he had a thoroughly good time, the question remained with him, almost forgotten, until later on it forced itself into his creative consciousness. In other ways, too, his freedom to travel has been important; in particular it has helped promote the cause of contemporary letters. For example, in May 1962, he served as leader of the British jury at the Formentor Literary Conference at Majorca, one of the most important international events of its kind. He has lectured in twenty-eight countries—more often abroad, it seems, than at home—and during his visit to the United States addressed university audiences at Yale, Harvard, Chicago, Los Angeles, and elsewhere. His lectures were warmly received and did much to en-lighten American understanding of the contemporary novel in England. At the same time, Wilson has responded with equal warmth to the cheerful spirit of his American hosts. He has not written another novel since *The Old Men at the Zoo*, completed just before his visit in 1960: but there is some reason to believe that his next work may reflect his encounters in that country. At least, Americans seem to have provided the sort of "healthful tonic for his anxious pessimism" that they have for John Wain. Or, at any rate, to so much Wilson has generously and publicly confessed.[8]

At present, Angus Wilson lives in a remote part of Suffolk where he can write and also do a little gardening. There and in London, where he maintains a small flat, he leads a very social life, "too social," he says, "for the work I have to do." But his activities show no sign of lessening. He has not again written for the stage, but has turned to television and radio drama while he continues to write fiction, book reviews, and commentaries upon English life. Most of these activities will be treated in the following chapters, but the emphasis will remain upon Wilson as an imaginative writer. Unlike his *Émile Zola*, this introductory study will not attempt a psychological analysis of the man and his work but a literary interpretation of the work itself—or of so much of the man as the writer may reveal. For, as Wilson elsewhere has said, "the text gives us the writer and it is from the writer's humanity that the critics must be fed."[9] "The text gives us the writer," and it is to these texts that we now turn.

REFERENCES

1. "The Whites in South Africa," 1961, p. 617.
2. "Bexhill and After," 1958, p. 583.
3. "The Naive Emancipator," 1955, p. 73.
4. "Bexhill and After," p. 584.
5. *W.W.*, p. 254.
6. See A. Jenkins, "Hemlock— and Before," *Spectator*, 1954, p. 331.
7. *W.W.*, p. 256.
8. "The Tragic View of Life," 1962, p. 22.
9. "'To Know and Yet Not to Fear Reality,'" 1955, p. 80.

CHAPTER II

THE WRONG SET AND
SUCH DARLING DODOS

The original, enthusiastic response to Wilson's first two collections of short stories, *The Wrong Set* and *Such Darling Dodos*, unquestionably owed much to their refreshing wit and vigorous satire. Causing this response, too, was the brilliant way that they treated the problems of contemporary life, particularly the difficulties of social re-adjustment in post-war England. They offered no panaceas, of course, but as John Wain has observed,[1] they had the merit of telling their readers something about the world they were then living in. If, a decade and a half later, they still hold both our interest as well as our admiration, we may have to look further to find some more solid basis for judgment. We shall see then, perhaps, that their ultimate appeal lies in a fundamental concern with recurrent human predicaments, like defeated pride or divided loyalty, rather than in an obvious ability to amuse or in an expert detailing of time and place. Finally, in their development of the short story form we may discover still another reason why these stories tend to remain among the more significant accomplishments of recent fiction.

For all the variety of individual experience, a number of rather clearly defined character types and situations emerge from among the twenty-three stories contained within these volumes. There is, for example, the Raffish Old Sport who appears in various stages of increasing decrepitude, like Trevor in the title story, "The Wrong Set," or Mr Nicholson in "Rex Imperator." Many of these studies seem to be modelled upon Wilson's own father and reflect a mixed attitude of affection and contempt. This ambivalence is typical of Wilson's attitude to many other characters, whose weaknesses he tries to understand without at the same time absolving them of blame for the evil they cause. Elspeth Eccles, the Intense Young Woman of "Fresh Air Fiend," Hamish Cockshutt and Donald Carrington, the Young Intellectuals in "Crazy Crowd" and "Mother's Sense of Fun," are other cases in point. Many of the characters deserve to be grouped under the semi-opprobrium of the titles of these collections, and often the titles of individual stories themselves provide ironic commentaries— "Saturnalia," "Realpolitik," "Sister Superior." But the characters are not really very far removed from what we may like to believe is normal, or at any rate actual, life. The titles of these collections, like the stories they are taken from, cut two ways.

Among the many character types, Wilson's interest is keenest where the type is most varied. Most significant is the Widow Who Copes. She reappears frequently, though not quite so often as the Raffish Old Sport; her experiences, however, are both more varied and more serious. Often, like Mrs Graham in "Heart of Elm" or Mary in "Sister Superior," she has children, a boy and a girl: but occasionally she is alone, like Thea in "Christmas Day at the Workhouse." Her experiences usually have much to do with the problem of fulfilling what remains of her life. Sometimes she shows an extreme possessiveness about her children (Mrs Carrington in "Mother's Sense of Fun"); at others she doggedly carries on in lonely but useful work (Thea's War service). In *The Middle Age of Mrs Eliot*, Wilson's most searching novel, the lives of three or four such widows enlighten Meg's, whose existence alters abruptly with the sudden loss of her husband. It thus becomes possible to treat Wilson's short stories as merely preliminary sketches for his novels—a temptation to which we easily enough succumb. But there is a question whether Wilson would ever have written novels had it not been for the success of his stories—a success which, as we have seen, he had neither anticipated nor planned on. In any case, though the novels may, and in fact do, grow naturally out of the stories, the latter still have a strong claim to be judged on their own merits.

Throughout *The Wrong Set* and *Such Darling Dodos*, no matter what kind of characters he portrays, Wilson seems primarily interested in the success or failure—or sheer unwillingness—of people to understand what they are and what they are doing. Because of this psychological or consciously analytical bias, symbolism is not one of his basic literary techniques. Where symbols appear, they are almost always explicitly translated, usually by the character whom they most concern. In "Significant Experience," for example, when Jeremy goes for a walk with Prue during the last day of their affair in the south of France, he sees in front of a villa an especially ornate garden whose rich flowers look faded, dust-covered, and dry. On the veranda sits an old woman in black; she, too, looks wan and dessicated. For Jeremy, this scene resembles the end of his exotic affair with an older woman, someone who is still quite attractive and very adept at love-making, but whose increasing possessiveness has begun to stifle him. When the description is over, explication follows directly: "The whole deadened spectacle connected in [Jeremy's] mind with his thoughts about Prue and he shuddered."[2] This is quite at the other extreme, say, from Joyce's technique in *Dubliners*. Elsewhere, the explication of symbolism may be part of an interior monologue; it is typical of Wilson's more alert characters that they should try to interpret their experiences to themselves in this way. Where Wilson's symbols remain unexplained, as in the storm that gathers over the picnickers in "Et Dona Ferentes,"

they are either so obvious or so deeply-rooted in the
story that an explanation would seriously hamper their
function—to say nothing of affronting the reader.

The situations Wilson treats of are invariably dramatic
and often, as in Ibsen's plays, begin at a point just
before a crisis.[3] A visit or some other intrusion into the
normal relationships of the characters—the loss of a
job, reorganisation of an office, death—usually precipitates the crisis. Because of the limitations of its form,
the short story can present only the most important
events leading up to the crisis, the crisis itself, and the
resulting shock: it has not the scope, as Wilson uses it,
for a follow-through, a gradual reconstruction of
attitudes or any other sustained denouement. And since
Wilson is most concerned with the dramatic impact of
these situations upon his central characters, he frequently
employs the interior monologue to investigate its consequences. He does not adopt the stream-of-consciousness
style of *Ulysses*, however, nor even the variation of it
that Virginia Woolf uses, although there are closer
similarities to her technique, perhaps, than to anyone
else's. Basically, Wilson's use of interior monologue
derives from such nineteenth-century writers as Émile
Zola, an admitted influence. In "Mother's Sense of
Fun," Donald Carrington's meditation as he lies in
bed listening to his mother talk with their cook illus-
trates how versatile the form can be, notwithstanding its
presentation in the third person.[4] In the space of a few
sentences, the narrator blends a report of information
with scraps of dialogue and even the direct personal
address of his main character. In other stories, like "Et
Dona Ferentes" and "Heart of Elm," Wilson introduces
the interior monologues of several characters. By contrasting the ways in which they all respond to a central
event, he develops a kind of psychological drama that
underlies or reinforces the surface drama carried forward by the dialogue.

Typically, Wilson's characters belong to either the declining middle classes between the Wars, or the rising lower classes and ascendant bureaucracies— academic bureaucracies included—of the nineteen-forties. What happens to such people is therefore his special concern, though not his limitation. "A Story of Historical Interest," for example, deals with shabby-genteel Lois Gorringe's self-sacrificing efforts to care for her widowed father, a Raffish Old Sport. When the old man suffers a stroke, Lois's efforts to nurse him reveal not only her own clumsiness and futility, but also her father's basic ingratitude for everything she has tried to do for him. Lois is deeply wounded, especially when Mr Gorringe prefers to stay in a cheap and rather un-likely nursing home rather than remain with her: but the shock is salutary. At the end, as his illness takes a serious turn for the worse, Lois refuses to come to his side; she looks forward instead to a party that evening and "the hundreds of interesting new people" she hopes to meet before going on to dinner with friends.

Lois Gorringe's response to her father's impending death may strike some readers as remarkably cold-blooded, particularly if they fail to see the bitterness that underlies her decision and the real effort that her bravado costs. But it is towards life that Lois turns, not towards the quagmires of sentimentality that have characterised her earlier experience. Her decision thus foreshadows the action of Wilson's later and more fully developed heroines. Living sometimes involves re-nunciation of what we have previously held dear, Wilson seems to say, especially when that something or some-one—like Mr Gorringe—has tended to drain rather than fulfill our highest potentialities for existence. But not all of the people in these stories are able to withstand the shock of such revelations. In "Fresh Air Fiend," Pro-fessor Searle collapses before the spectacle of his marriage that a pupil, Miss Eccles, has drawn for him. In "The

Wrong Set," an unhappy Vi, surrounded by the misery and squalor provided by her lover, who is off on a drunk, and a seedy nightclub job, from which she has just been fired, tries to get some of her own back. She telegraphs her sister that her son, who has earlier rebuffed Vi's attempts to be friendly, has fallen into the hands of communists, conchies, and Jews—the "wrong set," as she with unintended self-irony describes them. Even Rex Palmer's meagre triumph in "Rex Imperator" is seriously qualified by his emotional breakdown at the end of the story; it is left for his admiring wife to take charge and with calm matter-of-factness restore their household's equilibrium.

This element of pathos amidst disaster clearly attests to Wilson's generally humane point of view, and would seem to soften the misanthropy that many of his critics once charged him with (some still do). In the complex fabric of his design, pathos plays an important part, as it seldom does in the stories and novels of Evelyn Waugh, to whom he has most often been compared. Even in farcical situations—and in these stories Wilson, like Waugh, proves to be an excellent maker of farce—other dimensions, or depths, sometimes appear beneath the predominant hilarity. The farce that makes up almost the whole of "Saturnalia" is touched in this way as well as by more pointed stabs of satire. For example, when the hotel manageress, Mrs Hennessy, discharges a waitress because she is jealous of the attention Bruce Talfourd-Rich has shown her, she reveals a poverty of spirit not only in herself, but in her whole *milieu*, since Bruce is the shallowest sort of ladies' man—and a cad besides. A more sombre pathos darkens the uproarious family dinner in "Union Reunion" when the way Laura's son died finally becomes known. In "Toten-tanz" the farcical, the pathetic, and the grotesque all merge in the culminating disaster of Isobel Capper's first—and last—London entertainment, as suicide, murder, and other acts of despair rapidly follow one another to the end.

The violence at the end of "Totentanz" is, however, only an outward manifestation of the psychological violence that occurs frequently among Wilson's stories. In "The Wrong Set" or "Rex Imperator" no one actually dies or is killed, but a series of psychological outrages takes place that causes severe injuries of another order. A snub, among Wilson's characters, may be every bit as damaging as its physical counterpart, the knife wound. It is certainly intended to be. Stephanie's involuntary cruelty and Thea's retaliation in "Christmas Day at the Workhouse" are instances of such psychological warfare. If the violence is withstood—and sometimes it is ironically misunderstood, as at the end of "What Do Hippos Eat?"—the characters may come off stronger for having been subjected to it, toughened by the experience and often embittered by it, but at least better prepared for the ways of this world. Disaster lies either in being unaware of the violence taking place (Mary in "Sister Superior"), or in surrendering to it (John Hobday's staff in "Realpolitik"). But standing up to the revelation of violence has a danger of its own— the danger dramatised by Margaret Tarrant's ruthless pronouncement about her brother at the end of "A Visit in Bad Taste." There exists a frontier, Wilson suggests, on each side of our humanity: confronting reality too boldly, or not confronting it boldly enough, is to become either more or less than human.

But when everything else has been said, what emerges as Wilson's most salient characteristic in these stories is his histrionic sensibility, as demonstrated primarily by his use of dialogue. His ability to capture the sound of the human voice has justly been acclaimed by critics; only slightly less acclaimed is his ability to grasp the way people think. He is most successful with the types of people he has lived among: the dons of his Oxford

and British Museum days, the professional and mer-
cantile classes of his childhood, civil servants from the
Foreign Office, and the rest of the people—actors,
writers, editors—who make up his personal acquaintance.
It is the varied voice of middle-classdom, but occasionally
a lower-class accent appears, a cockney's, an East
Anglian farmer's, or some other. The settings of his
stories are never important in themselves, but are strictly
limited to introducing his characters' personalities. Thus
the main character in "Realpolitik," the new chief of a
provincial art gallery, is quite briefly presented, sitting
at the edge of his desk waiting for his staff to give him
their attention. Dialogue immediately follows, and in
John Hobday's opening remarks we soon recognise the
accents of the huckster, the Young Bureaucrat on the
Make. Through a series of slight interruptions by his
audience, we become aware almost as quickly that a
tense situation is developing between them.[5] The effect
of this presentation, as in most of Wilson's stories, is
exactly that of a curtain rising in a theatre. We are
propelled at once into a dramatic event, picking up
whatever information we need to understand it mainly
from the dialogue, but with the advantage, too, of
liberally supplied internal monologues. This is certainly
at the other extreme not only of Joyce, but of Joseph
Conrad or William Faulkner, who often share the
exposition and the action of their stories equally between
dialogue and description. In stories that deal chiefly
with the inner conflict of a single character, as in
"Raspberry Jam," Wilson also seems to prefer a rather
theatrical presentation. Thus before proceeding to
Johnnie's recollection of past events, he shows the boy
in the company of his mother and her circle, who play
only secondary roles in the story. Even in "A Little Companion," the objective, omniscient narrator passes quickly
from a few preliminary remarks to describe his subject,
Miss Arkwright, as she first appears during a cocktail party.

To introduce his stories, Wilson chooses such social gatherings as staff meetings, parties, family picnics or dinners, because they offer many opportunities for dialogue with which to begin at once the play and counterplay of human personality. His technique of defining a character or a group of characters by their reaction to a common event or to other characters is both quickly and easily employed. Here he seems to be following Joyce and Virginia Woolf, but of course earlier writers, such as Jane Austen and Dickens, whom Wilson much admires, developed the device as well.[6] Thus the encyclopaedists of "Learning's Little Tribute" first appear at the graveside of a deceased colleague, as each one manœuvres to profit from the sudden gap in their ranks. Later they reappear, trying to prevent their chief from making the situation serve his own interest. Finally, all of them are brought face to face with their colleague's widow, whose honest and independent spirit, together with her genuine feelings of bereavement, baffles their condescension and frustrates the aims of their charity. Such an arrangement of incidents suggests a dance-like movement, or structure, which becomes still more apparent in "Totentanz," as the title partly suggests. A less ordered dance, thoroughly in keeping with its theme, appears in "Saturnalia." In "A Flat Country Christmas" (first published in 1950 as "Old, Old Message" but not collected until later), this analogy between the sequence of events and a dance is made explicit.[7] But the intricacies of a dance do not justify the rather mechanical arrangement of incidents in "Realpolitik" or the serial re-telling of events in "Mother's Sense of Fun"—stories which depend much more for their effect than the others upon a final ironic twist or shock. In *For Whom the Cloche Tolls: A Scrap-Book of the Twenties* (1953), Wilson achieves his *tour de force*, complete with drawings by Philippe Jullian. He again begins with a death, but unlike "Learning's Little Tribute," here the dead person becomes the central figure. In the story, related mainly by letters, Maisie's children, friends, and others record their reactions to her death but more importantly to her life, especially those aspects of her life which appear to epitomise the spirit of her age. The technique is of course Jamesian, which may have something to do with the heroine's American birth as well as her name. At the end, her own voice is briefly heard—in excerpts from a diary—but brief as it is, it becomes the fitting culmination for the whole presentation of her character and her epoch.

At his best, then, Wilson presents an intricate drama of tense personal relationships. These often may be diagrammed (though not without violence to the closely-woven fabric of his design) by a triangular pattern, or several superimposed triangular patterns. At the base of the triangle is usually a couple in a relationship of either harmony or tension, as in "Fresh Air Fiend" or "A Visit in Bad Taste." At the apex, exerting pressure upon either or both of the principals at the base, is a third person—or group of persons, as in "A Story of Historical Interest" or "What Do Hippos Eat?" As conflict grows, the triangle may be seen to invert itself, the point of the apex now becoming a wedge forcing apart the couple at the base. In more complex situations, the number of triangular situations usually increases. The essential thing, however, is to recognise the human drama of these stories, whether it involves the almost wholly introverted conflict of "Necessity's Child," or the outward conflicts of a large group of people. In those stories which deal with a few people—no more than three or four—Wilson appears to probe most deeply, using his most incisive irony. Very possibly his greatest achievements in fiction lie in this direction. But no one can deny his other achievements, especially his handling of farce, which invariably requires the management of many more persons; and in his novels an important part of the action—like the hilarious opening of Vardon Hall in *Hemlock and After* or Marie-Hélène's "do" in *Anglo-Saxon Attitudes*—reaches its climax in this way.

A detailed analysis of one of the stories may be useful here. "Heart of Elm" is a likely choice since it deals with characteristic themes and situations, and since its structure falls somewhere between the single triangular pattern described above and the more complex structure of stories having a larger cast of persons. It begins with the dialogue of Constance Graham, a widow, and her two children, Thomas and Katherine. In a room upstairs the children's old nurse, Ellen, lies dying. Constance is busy preparing sandwiches for the three or four members of Ellen's family who will presently arrive, separately, to pay their last—and almost only—respects to their sister. The children deeply resent this intrusion into their household; they are afraid that at the last moment they will be displaced in the affections of their dear nurse. This is especially true of Katherine, the intense young teen-ager whose tight-lipped heroism is almost more than her older brother can bear: for Thomas, "capacity for self-expression is not incompatible with true feeling."[8] But the narrator's comments swiftly undercut the pretensions of both children, directing our sympathies instead towards their mother, who actually looks forward to Ellen's death. She longs to sell the house which has been a veritable prison to her, and in the ten years or so that remain of her middle age, she wants to live by herself in London. As for her offspring, Constance resents their lingering adolescence. She believes that Ellen is mainly responsible for it, although she recognises that she must share in the responsibility too, partly because of her initial blindness, and partly because of her unwillingness afterwards to alter the situation by hurting others. The time has come, however, when she must act decisively—or lose everything. Summoning up courage to take her stand, she confronts the children with her plans before the guests arrive. Thomas and Katherine are, in their own ways, naturally shocked by the decision; then they are almost horrified by the revelations about themselves and their relationship with Ellen that Constance is forced to make. Before this conflict can be resolved, or, indeed, proceed further, the first visitor drives up to the house.

So far, the general pattern of relationships is fairly simple. Ellen, representing the life of their childhood, lies in harmonious but now delicate balance with Katherine and Thomas. Constance, at the apex of the triangle, appears to exert pressure downwards on either side, when suddenly, as Ellen is dying, she becomes a wedge-like force breaking up the relationship at the base. The arrival of Jack Gilmore, Ellen's black-sheep brother, inaugurates a series of new relationships which not only increases the complexities of the drama, but culminates in the ironic turn of events at the end.

Jack's success in cheering Ellen up at once poses a double threat: bringing out the coarser side of Ellen's nature, he transforms the image the children wish to retain of their simple old nurse; and Thomas, at least, suspects that Mr Gilmore will try to inveigle whatever he can of Ellen's property—a threat real enough, but of only secondary importance in the story. Gilmore thus momentarily replaces Constance at the apex of the triangle, forcing apart the children's bond with Ellen, and suggesting a regrouping of relationships that will eventually lump all the Grahams together as against the members of Ellen's own family.

The second guest is Mrs Temple, Ellen's younger sister, who arrives with her son, Len. Mrs Temple's comic, genteel affectation somewhat reduces the tension generated so far, as Ellen receives her shortly and immediately pretends to sleep. At this point, Constance asks her son to take charge of their guests. He delights in putting himself over these people, and climaxes his "performance" with the invention of an appropriate epithet for Ellen: "She is, you know, a real heart of oak." The histrionics, the sentimentality of the phrase, immediately unite everyone in a splendid show of appreciation (Constance of course is absent, and we are not sure where Katherine is). But the feeling is short-lived. Lottie, Ellen's older, unmarried sister, arrives and at once takes full command of things, leaving Constance, Thomas, and Katherine to sit alone in the hall, waiting for the end.

When the end does come, it introduces a new and thoroughly ironic perspective. For it is in Constance's arms that the old nurse chooses to die, mumbling, "My dearie, my lovie." The effect upon Mrs Graham is one of complete horror. Ellen's last gesture would seem to defeat her again, destroying at one stroke her hard won determination to escape: "it was clearly she whom Ellen had adored," she says to herself, "she could not deceive herself about that, however stiffly she had held the dying woman, she knew that she was holding the person who had loved her more than anyone ever would, and that calculatedly she must betray that love."[9] This love, invisible even to its chief object, has underlain all the others. But Constance, like many of Wilson's heroines, shows strength enough to maintain her earlier resolve. Her renunciation of Ellen's love reveals a tragic awareness that may seem harsh, cruel, and bitter: yet it must also seem brave. The story tries to make this point explicit. At the end, in a deliberate anti-climax of mingled farce and pathos, Constance seizes upon the undertaker's recommendation to use elm wood for Ellen's coffin. She begins to laugh and explains, "I was only just thinking—not heart of *oak*, you know, at all, heart of *elm*." When Katherine tries to interpret the remark favourably, describing Ellen as "a great elm under which we all sheltered," Constance does not allow

c

her to be entirely deceived. "Oh! yes," she says, "she was like an elm tree. But understand this, there aren't any more elm trees, no more hearts of elm."[10]

Some years ago, in a review article for *The Spectator*, Wilson surveyed the development of the short story in the twentieth century. Against the "classic" story of Somerset Maugham's era, he contrasted Katherine Mansfield's attempts to inject "greater subtlety of mood and deeper levels of consciousness" into a form that had hitherto emphasised narrative and surprise. The result was almost to destroy the short story by reducing it to a "sketch." More recently, writers have tried to combine these elements into a single form. Novelists have faced a similar problem, but Wilson believes that, on the whole, the short story writers have been more successful "in restoring shape without losing subtlety."[11] However we may agree or disagree with these conclusions, especially the last, one fact about Wilson's own stories remains clear. He certainly has contributed much towards restoring the classic form of the earlier era. His influence is especially significant in the use of dramatic techniques to convey his narrative, as we have seen. His influence in the novel is similar, although there he succeeds somewhat more perfectly in keeping the balance between narrative action and deeper levels of consciousness.

REFERENCES

1. "Comment on Widowhood," *The New Yorker*, XXXV, 11 Apr. 1959, p. 164.
2. *W.S.*, p. 165.
3. Cp. Ian Scott-Kilvert, "Angus Wilson," 1960, p. 44.
4. *W.S.*, pp. 188–9.
5. *W.S.*, p. 63.
6. Cp. *W.W.*, p. 260.
7. *B.O.M.*, pp. 42–5.
8. *S.D.D.*, p. 180.
9. *S.D.D.*, p. 196.
10. *S.D.D.*, p. 197.
11. "The Short Story Changes," 1954, p. 401.

CHAPTER III

HEMLOCK AND AFTER

"Humanism is dead; long live humanism!"—this, says A. O. J. Cockshut,[1] might well be the motto for Angus Wilson's first novel, *Hemlock and After*. Indeed it might; and if Mr Cockshut elsewhere in his essay misconstrues some points, he has here touched upon a theme present in all of Wilson's novels. The humanism of Bernard Sands in *Hemlock and After* fails because it has at its heart a radical self-deception: it screens off the uglier kinds of human motive and behaviour and pretends to qualify its acts of otherwise pure altruism with only the most enlightened or innocuous self-interest. Although this humanism eventually appears to do others some good, it fails Bernard after the façade is lifted, for there is nothing powerful enough in it—or in him (hence his surname)—upon which he can base his future existence. Reconstruction after insight becomes the goal of Wilson's next two novels: but in *Hemlock and After* we are presented mainly with the terrible self-revelation that confronts the chief character and leads to his despair.

The novel begins with Bernard Sands's most recent— and for him, most significant—public triumph: the establishment at Government expense of Vardon Hall, a haven for young writers. Himself a novelist and former schoolmaster, Bernard has long championed the cause of liberal and independent thinking under the banners of what he calls anarchic humanism. Authority, especially in its restrictive, complacent, self-important aspects, looms as his enemy; and in the pose of a latter-day Socrates, Bernard enjoys twitting it as often and as sharply as he can. His present success has its particular pleasure since he has at last met authority "at its most impersonal level"[2] and won from it a victory almost totally free of conditions. Not only will Vardon Hall provide leisure and support for young writers, but it will not be burdened by any of the forms of external control that many have sought to impose. Bernard is undoubtedly right in advocating freedom for the writers that they may grow of their own accord; he is, furthermore, to be admired for resisting the control over his scheme that others would regard as his due. But his enjoyment of the chagrin and even outrage he causes local and state dignitaries by winning on his own terms shows a mixed motive in his action, the implications of which he is soon painfully compelled to recognise.

Cutting now into Bernard's reflexions of guarded self-satisfaction, and breaking his mood, comes the voice of his wife. Ella's deeply neurotic state contrasts strongly with his appearance and represents for him failure of an intensely personal kind. It is only slightly less acute than the failure he shares with her in the upbringing of their children, James and Elizabeth. The first incident in the novel, in fact, counterpoints Bernard's private failures and his public successes, and is developed more thoroughly at the cocktail party given for him that afternoon by James and his wife, Sonia. In the course of the novel, Ella emerges as certainly the most important of a number of significant parallels and contrasts to Bernard: but she poses some problems for the reader because she is not fully enough drawn. Anticipating a bit, we may say that she, rather than Bernard, is the real hero of the novel, or rather shows the greater heroism. Though Wilson inadequately explores the wellsprings of this heroism, she provides the clearest link to the heroism shown in his later novels.

As the Sandses prepare to go to their son's party, Bernard becomes aware of his growing preoccupation with—and apprehension of—the nature of evil. Shortly afterwards, Ella and he drive past the cottage of Mrs Curry who, more than just another person in the novel, comes to represent for Bernard (as she does for Wilson) the very embodiment of evil.[3] Beyond her lust for money and for men, and beyond the "endless malevolence" peeping through her elephantine figure and the cloying sweetness of her demeanour, Bernard senses "a sprawling waste of energy in malice for its own sake that could not be quite satisfactorily dismissed as thwarted power."[4] She is a "natural destroyer," he concludes, "pitted against life itself." So, too, is Sherman Winter, and others, he feels, whose undisguised viciousness makes hypocrisy—while still deeply distasteful to him—not an essential part of his growing conception of evil. His thoughts abruptly turn then to the favourable reviews of his recent novel, *The Player Queen*. He dismisses his earlier meditation as merely the result of nervous anxiety, and begins to contemplate the pleasure of disappointing his son and daughter-in-law and their friends who hope that now he will finally live up to his position and be the Grand Old Man of Letters. He fails to see that in this action (which is duly carried forward) lies an element of the same destructiveness which moments ago he had condemned in Mrs Curry and Sherman Winter. But if Bernard is not guilty of hypocrisy, he is clearly guilty of self-deception. His malice, unlike the others', is so well hidden from his eyes that he can seriously play the part of a morally enlightened person trying to instruct others by puncturing their self-importance and thereby upsetting the petty tyrannies of their neo-authoritarianism.

Not that James and Sonia, and most of their guests, do not deserve such treatment, and perhaps worse. James, a barrister, is an insufferable prig and his wife a vicious young predator willing to injure anyone, even the helpless Ella, to satisfy her longing for limelight—

or to relieve her frustrations when limelight is denied. Their gathering of friends and neighbours provides an excellent sampling of the kinds of people that have characterised the home counties and other suburban areas since the Second World War. Lawyers, gentlemen-farmers, young stockbrokers, together with their snobbish wives, are all assembled here, revealing the social pressures and quasi-intellectual forces which the younger generation share and against which Bernard battles. The arrangement is very much like one of Wilson's short stories, but the implications go further. At one point, for instance, James turns in disgust from his father's gadfly behaviour towards Mrs Rankine, a local lady hopelessly ruined by her reading of Virginia Woolf. He sees beneath his father's pretence of universal understanding, of his "Dostoevskeyan emotional brotherhood," a basic contempt for most of humanity. By contrast, he applauds himself and his wife for their "civilized tolerance" of the vulgar stupidity largely in evidence to them also. In so doing, however, James betrays his own self-deception, a pharisaical attitude that derives simultaneously from a refusal to "understand humanity" and a conviction about legal justice. "If people were too weak or too stupid to cope with life as it was, then they had to be taught," he concludes, completely oblivious of any irony in his position.[5]

During this episode we also learn the nature of Ella's neurosis, of the extreme difficulty she has escaping from her paranoid prison to establish any satisfactory communion with others. The imagery of frozen underground seas and the grappling hooks of exterior stimuli vividly and dramatically describes her plight. Though it is not until nearly the end of the novel that the causes of her condition are explained[6]—they are nowhere *presented*—though, in short, we must accept her condition as a *donnée*—her illness is nevertheless convincing. Her startling recovery just before Bernard's death is another matter: implausible on dramatic grounds, whatever the psychological possibility, it is otherwise accounted for by the book's basic thematic development. Ella's inability to establish satisfactory human contact is only the most obvious example of this predicament in the novel: others, including Bernard, share it even if they remain largely unaware of it or, unlike Ella, less obsessed by it. The breakdown of personal communications agrees well with the theme of self-knowledge, is an extension of it or perhaps a necessary corollary, if we view the problem within its complete human context.[7]

Thus when Elizabeth confronts her father the next day with her knowledge of his recent homosexual behaviour, their meeting ends disastrously. It is not the less disastrous when Bernard is disturbed by her characteristic attitude of "brightly disguised boredom with life" and wishes to help.[8] Forced to defend his own actions, he describes his personal life as something he knows must pain both him and his family but also as something chiefly concerning himself, and of only incidental or secondary concern to his wife and children. Elizabeth recognises the cold justice of this analysis; Bernard, however, forfeits any claim to her sympathies when, afraid of responding directly and immediately to the anguish he has caused her, he tries to shift the conversation to her other problems. The artificiality of his approach exasperates his daughter, and "the tough wall of failed contact and resentment"[9] that exists between them, that stood for a moment some chance of being broken through, is instead reinforced. The failure of their dialogue, moreover, is related, as Elizabeth senses, to the largely theoretical nature of Bernard's humanism, to its lack of immediate human relevance, which, when it finally crashes around him, falls because of this failure of direct human touch.

However much it is a drain on his strength, Bernard's failure with his family does not represent his most

intense personal involvements, or, eventually, his most
depressing defeats. These concern other relationships
of responsibility: for example, with Terence Lambert,
his first homosexual lover, to whom he is still devoted;
and with Eric Craddock, a boy he thinks gifted and is
trying to liberate from the iron clamps of his mother.
It is here that Bernard sustains the greatest attacks upon
the image of himself as a benevolent if somewhat acid-
tongued reformer. He begins to realise that his pose
rings hollow in others' ears, especially those nearest to
him, as both Eric and Terence reject not the substance
of his morality, but his moralising attitude. Play-acting—
deliberate or habitual histrionics—in fact characterises
many of those who inhabit Bernard's world. Eric's
narcissistic day-dreaming, his mother's more calculating
assumption of roles, the Edwardian posturing of a
neighbour, Hubert Rose, all sharpen his—and our—
awareness of this danger. So do Bernard's sister, Isobel
Sands, a professor of English addicted to left-wing
politics, and his brother-in-law, Bill Pendlebury, a fat,
failing biographer with an enormous capacity for high-
sounding nonsense. In their different ways, they try
Bernard's soul; he feels that he lives "in a world of
never-grow-ups" who are useless in politics and everywhere else that clarity of vision and the disinterested
exercise of power are required.[10] His suspicions about
them, though, are but outward reflexions of what he has
lately begun to suspect about himself. His latest novel,
The Player Queen, thus by its very title suggests deeper
and more terrible self-ironies than any of those he had
originally directed against others.[11]

The climactic blow against Bernard's image of himself follows a rapid series of shocks begun by Elizabeth
and continued through Terence's announcement that he
is giving up his flat to live with Sherman Winter, a
vicious kind of bloodsucker. Bernard, hoping to dissuade
Terence, waits for him one evening in Leicester Square.

Brooding upon the theme of "the proper use of authority" introduced at dinner by his friend Charles Murley, an important and dedicated civil servant, he suddenly awakens to the voice of a police detective asking him to offer evidence of importuning against a young man. He refuses, but is frozen with horror at his own "hunter's thrill" until Terence arrives and huddles him into a taxi.

The screens of evasion which his beneficent humanism had seemed to construct around the more sinister aspects of his nature here finally collapse, leaving Bernard face to face with what he had long suspected in others but would not or could not see in himself. The central irony of the novel, which Cockshut misconceives, is thus to bring Bernard closer in line with other characters, like Eric's mother or Mrs Curry, who likewise are guilty of false motives or even deliberate malice. According to Cockshut,[12] when Bernard emerges similarly tainted, Wilson unfairly exalts him above the rest by reason only of his greater awareness of the evil that is in him. But since Bernard alone has ever claimed any moral superiority, his confrontation of his faults is necessarily more terrible—and more brave.[13] He no longer justifies his teasing Eric or provoking Terence as useful techniques of instruction, but sees in them only his desire for sadistic pleasure.[14] His self-condemnation is even more severe and thorough-going. At the opening of Vardon Hall a few days after the Leicester Square incident, he observes the calculated mischief of his enemies and the dignity of the official speakers. "Among this whole crowd," he muses, "he thought himself alone, the coward who had refused to face the dual nature of all human action, whose resplendent, eccentric cloak of broadminded, humane, individual conduct had fallen to pieces in one moment under the glaring neon searchlight of that single test of his humanity in Leicester Square. He had failed the test and must take the consequences."[15]

Power corrupts; absolute power corrupts absolutely. But Bernard's refusal to assume any power at all has dangers of its own, he discovers. The "cloak of broad-minded, humane, individual conduct" becomes simply a form of irresponsibility, for which he is criticised by various characters in the book—unduly by his son James, but quite properly by others like Charles Murley. Aversion to responsibility, disguising itself in informality or easy-going *laissez-faire*, also explains Bernard's failure as a father.[16] With Elizabeth he could defend himself against injuring his family on the basis that "Harm to others is after all implicit in most decisions we take,"[17] but he could do so only because his family's feelings had ceased to matter much to him. To the extent that their pain thus became less real, he could dismiss his part in causing it by such high-sounding apologies. Significantly, after the Leicester Square incident, it is the harm done to Terence and Eric that troubles him most. For Bernard never really accepts the dual nature of all human action; at best he but dimly perceives the streak of cruelty or sadism that underlies his humanist pose. To a man less usually aware of the complexity of the human heart (witness his scrutiny of himself and Mrs Craddock during their first meeting),[18] or to one less committed to his beliefs, the sudden realisation would hardly be so crippling. But for Bernard, the consequences are to propel him into an extremely critical examination of human motives, particularly his own motives, which receive curious and outrageous public exposure during his Vardon Hall speech. Like T. S. Eliot's Becket, he becomes aware that not only doing the right thing, but doing it for the right reason, is fundamental to the true exercise of virtue. Unable to free himself from the grip of this obsessive concern, he falls into a profound melancholia and paralysis of the will that ends only with his death. For Bernard, the hemlock he drinks is the knowledge of his own soul.

Wilson's first novel does not end, however, with unqualified pessimism. Though Bernard dies unable to piece together the fragments of his former self with the substance of his new insight, others go on living and are the better for their contact with him. Even he makes some attempt to redeem himself by acting to free a fifteen-year-old girl from the trap in which Mrs Curry will present her to Hubert Rose, whose despair contrasts with Bernard's and is also more vicious. Just before her husband's heart attack, Ella makes her own startling recovery. If her recovery is dramatically implausible, it nevertheless demonstrates an effort of will that is both perilous and courageous. As such, it complements the failure of Bernard's will, fulfilling a capacity for heroism that he, physically and morally undermined, cannot. The crucial test of her humanity comes after the Vardon Hall fiasco. Responding to the task, the duty, the call on her love provided by Bernard's problems and their unresolved state after his death, she carries forward the plans that they had begun to formulate on the eve of his fatal heart attack. Not all of her actions, of course, achieve their goals, or achieve them altogether. The catastrophe that besets Vardon Hall—the arrival of the sort of petty tyrant Bernard hated—is a final irony. But able to hurt as well as help, or rather to help even as it necessarily involves paining others, Ella succeeds best of all in assisting Eric to free himself from his mother—just as Bernard would have wished but himself became incapable of doing from scruples about motive. Again, when she, unlike her husband, tries to help their daughter overcome a distaste for life, she accepts a momentary defeat—and tries again. This acceptance takes the form not only of intelligent self-criticism, but includes the highest tribute to her husband, with which the book ends. To Elizabeth's complaints about his ineffectual life, Ella replies that "doing doesn't last." "But Bernard *was* something to people," she continues,

"—lots of people—me, for example—and that has its effect in the end, I think."[19]

All of the talents for dialogue, farce, the dramatic presentation of characters, and a tightly knit ordering of incident that Wilson exhibits in his short stories are fully exploited in *Hemlock and After*. His evident wish to investigate more fully the inner workings of his characters is also satisfied, at least in Bernard Sands. The attempt to examine other characters with comparable fullness is less successful. Ella is too sketchily drawn, and of Terence Lambert, also, we should like to know more, or perhaps less: his rather unfinished portrait nags at the reader, since the depths behind it are suggested and to some extent dramatised, but otherwise poorly established. Like Ella's illness, they have to be taken as a *donnée*, from which follows his logical and consistent presentation. What has made him different from the golden haired spivs that congregate at Evelyn Rammage's party? Contact with Bernard is the only explanation offered, and it is only explanation: of their life together we have only a handful of reported fragments. All of this suggests the major artistic flaw in Wilson's first novel: the fabric of his design is so tightly drawn that a few gaps and bulges inevitably show through.

In other respects, *Hemlock and After* is a significant development from the short stories. However fragmentary some of the characterisations may appear, Wilson has conceived the basic structure of his novel with the eye of a master craftsman. All of Books One and Two, or about two-thirds of the novel, occupy the period of a single week in June 1951; the events of Book Three occur mostly in the week or two afterwards. Each book has its appropriate climax, but the peak of the entire structure comes during the opening of Vardon Hall in Book Two, in Bernard's public confession of his sins and in the wild farce that is then precipitated by his enemies

—Mrs Curry, Sherman Winter, Mrs Craddock, and the rest. As in his short stories, Wilson approaches the major crisis of Bernard's life from a point just before it occurs. But the greater latitude of the novel permits him to explore the causes of the crisis far more fully and deeply, and to introduce an impressive number of parallel and contrasting characters with which to develop his major themes. Hubert Rose's despair, for example, assumes the form of a profound cynicism both leading to and fed by his particular vice; his suicide shows him more abjectly and completely defeated than Bernard ever was. Bill Pendlebury's despair is pathetic rather than sinister; at the end of the novel he emerges basically unchanged, despite his assistance to Ella in sending Mrs Curry to jail (for which his sister gives him an income as a reward for his pains and as a token of her incredibly unshaken belief in his writing). Ella's recovery is in direct contrast to these despairs as well as to Bernard's but something should be said also of Terence Lambert's recovery from two self-deceptions: first, from his idyllic affair with Elizabeth Sands and the mistaken belief that it could lead to a new life for them both; secondly, from his idea that living with Sherman Winter could in any way advance his professional ambitions without destroying him as a person. As part of the affirmative tendency that counterbalances despair and defeat at the end of the novel (and connects with much of Wilson's later work), these renunciations have an essential function.

Of course, striking a proper balance between the demands of thematic development and characterisation for its own sake remains a problem in any novel, especially a long one. If in this short novel Wilson too completely subordinates his characterisations, it is probable that, although there has obviously been much progress, he has not yet fully emerged from the habits or limitations of the short story form. More progress will be necessary, but not only in filling out characters.

A subtler blending of incidents is also needed to link together chapters and even divisions within the chapters so that they do not appear as short stories somehow embedded within the novel. This criticism is particularly appropriate to the earlier chapters of *Hemlock and After*, where Wilson attempts to provide exposition in his usual dramatic form. In his next novel, *Anglo-Saxon Attitudes*, he tries to remedy both of these defects of under-development and structural transition. But even there he is still feeling his way towards the more complete unity of form and ideas that he achieves in *The Middle Age of Mrs Eliot*.

REFERENCES

1. "Favored Sons; The Moral World of Angus Wilson," 1959, p. 60.
2. *H.A.*, p. 11.
3. *W.W.*, p. 261.
4. *H.A.*, p. 15.
5. *H.A.*, p. 22.
6. *H.A.*, p. 227.
7. See also C. B. Cox, "The Humanism of Angus Wilson: A Study of *Hemlock and After*," 1961, pp. 229–231.
8. *H.A.*, pp. 55 ff.
9. *H.A.*, p. 59; cp. pp. 114, 124.
10. *H.A.*, p. 74.
11. See *H.A.*, p. 16 and cp. p. 188.
12. Cockshut, *op. cit.*, pp. 52–5.
13. For another reply to Cockshut, see Cox, *op. cit.*, p. 235.
14. *H.A.*, p. 189.
15. *H.A.*, p. 146.
16. *H.A.*, p. 215.
17. *H.A.*, p. 58.
18. *H.A.*, pp. 78 ff.
19. *H.A.*, p. 246.

CHAPTER IV

ANGLO-SAXON ATTITUDES

In a very real sense, *Anglo-Saxon Attitudes* begins just before *Hemlock and After* ends, with the despair of the principal character. Gerald Middleton—retired history professor, amateur art collector, sensualist, failed father, and husband living apart from his wife—leads an existence almost stifling in its sense of defeat brought about by evasion in both his personal and his professional life. But as Wilson elsewhere says,[1] his new hero learns that he must—and can—face up to the truth about his evasions; or rather, that he must face up to the truth about his professional responsibility, and the *result* of his not facing the truth about his responsibility to his family. By thus separating the issues, Wilson apparently wishes to clarify the ambiguous ending of *Hemlock and After*, that is, to distinguish between the realms in which doing has some necessary and useful effect, and those in which it does not or can not.[2] In this way, he tries to discover for his hero some kind of salvation from despair which will permit him to live, some pleasure principle—to use Wilson's own Freudian terms[3]—as against the working of an oppressive Calvinist conscience. The result is successful, and at the end of *Anglo-Saxon Attitudes* Gerald Middleton emerges with a renewed will to live. But his gains are not without serious and costly losses, especially in his personal relationships with his family, and with others.

The novel opens in Gerald's Montpelier Square flat on a morning a few days before Christmas 1953. Gerald's wife, Ingeborg, has telephoned earlier concerning the

family's annual Christmas reunion, and his housekeeper gives Gerald the message at breakfast. The news
annoys him since he does not relish speaking to his
wife on the telephone and he dreads the family Christmas.
The morning papers and letters further aggravate his
depressed state. Thumbing through a daily tabloid, he
is irritated by the histrionics of his younger son, John, a
former Labour M.P. now turned crusading journalist.
An inquiry from an American Ph.D. student seeking
information about his association with the poet Gilbert
Stokesay also bothers him, particularly as the inquirer
wants information about his friend's part in the Melpham
excavations of 1912. These were undertaken by Gilbert's
father, Professor Lionel Stokesay, and the question of
Gilbert's role is one Gerald has for years sought to evade.
The inquiry antagonises him, too, since it reminds him
of his ruined happiness with Dollie Stokesay, Gilbert's
widow. Finally, Sir Edgar Iffley's letter asking him to
assume the editorship of the *University Medieval History*
threatens to cause unpleasantness when Gerald realises
that he may have to insist upon staying professionally
inactive. Most of all, what depresses Gerald is "the
tediously repetitive chain of self-recrimination"[4] that
these meditations arouse and that intensifies his feelings
of distaste and self-disgust.

Wilson introduces the major aspects of Gerald's life
with his usual swift facility, focusing in this first chapter
mainly upon his character's professional career. The
interconnexions between Gerald's private and professional life also receive attention as, for example, Gerald
checks his criticism of his son's crusading after truth by
recalling that his own evasions allow him no such license.
A similar check motivates his refusal to help either the
Ph.D. candidate or Sir Edgar. For years Gerald has kept
to himself the disquieting suspicion of fraud that he alone
has felt regarding the excavation of Bishop Eorpwald's
tomb and the curious pagan idol found in it. His silence

derives from his feelings of personal obligation to the Stokesay family, and from his fear of hurting them or their reputations now that only Dollie survives. This evasion has influenced his own career as an historian and as a man, for he characteristically backs away from any call whatever upon powers he may once have had: his long-awaited book on Edward the Confessor is still largely unwritten, and he lacks even the courage of his sensual lusts. At sixty-four, he regards himself as that pitiful thing, a scholar with a great future behind him and—to add to the pity—a failure of the "most boring kind, a failure with a conscience."[5]

The technique of parallel or contrasting development of character and situation in *Hemlock and After* cuts an extraordinarily wide swath in *Anglo-Saxon Attitudes*, for multiplying the "worlds" of the novel as much as possible is Wilson's intention.[6] Hence, Gerald's wasted life is immediately compared to the wasted energies of still another historian and pupil of Professor Stokesay, Dr Rose Lorimer. But the preoccupation with Melpham that influences Gerald's life takes a more sinister turn with her. Although she was not present, like him, at the excavations, she has been profoundly moved by the unique mixture of paganism and Christianity that the excavations reveal. Thus she advocates the theory that compromise with paganism aided the Roman Catholic conversion of England and defeated the Church of Iona. This theory has become her *idée fixe*, resulting in various eccentricities of behaviour and ultimately threatening her sanity. After a lecture at the Historical Society, however, Professor Pforzheim, a noted German scholar, indicates that excavations in Heligoland may turn up evidence to support Professor Stokesay's discoveries. The news provides Rose with a deep sense of personal and professional vindication. She apparently gets over her dementia and engages upon a new life of far less hysterically motivated scholarship.

D

Dr Lorimer's recovery is anticipated by Gerald's, but both recoveries remain tentative until the foundations upon which they rest are challenged and shown sufficient. Rose's proves woefully inadequate, and she finally has to be certified. Gerald's is a more complicated affair, and many intertwining strands of the "tortured web" of his depression and despair must be unravelled and then tested, each separately, before he is completely free. The initial process of unravelling takes place on Christmas Eve at Marlow. Unwanted but persistent mental associations connect key phrases from his family's conversation with events of his past and force him to retrace his life, crisis by anguished crisis, until he has entirely relived the experiences that have led to his present frame of mind. The long *recherche* begins with Lionel Stokesay's political activities in 1939, as Gerald tries to dissuade him from persevering in actions which more and more tend to make him appear ludicrous. As Stokesay's "gas balloon" mounts higher, Gerald reacts with increasing distaste from his own once high aspirations. The next recollections centre upon Gerald's disastrous personal life. With disingenuous regularity, they move backwards in time from his last agonising encounter with Dollie to the origins of their prolonged and once happy love affair. The central issue concerns Gerald's marriage. After his three children are born, Dollie and he resume a love affair broken off earlier mainly because of Dollie's unresolved guilt over her dead husband and her still living and generous father-in-law. But though he finds happiness again with Dollie, Gerald has refused to sacrifice what he mistakenly conceives to be his duty to his family. He does not realise that his double life, despite the trappings of its evidently "sensible" arrangement, cannot last, that it must inevitably destroy every aspect of his happiness, depriving him eventually of both Dollie's love and his children's devotion. For anyone as sensitive as Dollie, the masquerade of her life with Gerald—allowing Ingeborg to pose as her friend, and acting as "Auntie" to the children—demands too great a sacrifice of pride, even of self-respect. Resentment then follows Gerald's initial blindness, only to be met by Dollie's increasing possessiveness. Their relationship finally becomes intolerable when Dollie's almost deliberate dipsomania forces a complete breaking-off.

The failure of Gerald's marriage, which in part leads to his double life, is of course largely a consequence of its unpropitious beginning. As his marriage deteriorates, Gerald, fed by springs of guilt, allows his wife foolishly to supervise the management of their household and the upbringing of their children. A hopeless sentimentalist, Ingeborg insists upon giving up servants and living within a strict economy while Gerald is merely a lecturer at the University, although their more than ample income can easily afford them a larger house and at least a nurse. Through her ineptitude (not without a suspicious trace of malice), Ingeborg once even causes their small daughter, Kay, to burn her hand and thus become permanently disfigured. Guilt, pity, and some ill-judged advice from a young doctor effectively prevent Gerald from probing more deeply into the "accident" and drive him still further from assuming full paternal responsibility. This abdication of responsibility increases during his affair with Dollie: but instead of seeking a divorce, he insists on remaining titular head of the family, deluding himself that he is sacrificing the lesser good—his happiness and Dollie's—to the greater good of his wife and children. No deception, of course, could be worse, either for his own welfare or for that of his family; and in this behaviour he seems not terribly far removed from the gross sentimentalities of his wife. Ironically, the guilt that motivates his actions and inhibits him from honestly confronting the situation is a function of the same mental attitude that in other ways proves unusually perceptive. But, like Bernard Sands, Gerald is not quite perceptive enough; or rather, his innate fear of hurting others causes him similarly to erect screens of evasion with which to cover over this basic weakness in his character.

The insight Gerald now gains by reliving these scenes of growing enstrangement from Dollie and his family is salutary; so, too, is his recollection of two scenes—the last in the series—which have to do with Melpham. The first takes place in 1914 with Gilbert Stokesay and is the source of Gerald's gravest doubts. In an habitual tirade against his father, Gilbert drunkenly reveals that the pagan idol found in Eorpwald's tomb, however authentic, was something deliberately put there by himself with the help of one of the workers as a kind of mammoth practical joke. He hopes to reveal the hoax on some public occasion when the truth may cause his father the greatest possible embarrassment. The cruelty of the prank—if prank it can be called—fits in with the perverse nature of this strange and brilliant young man; moreover, Gerald recalls "a sudden instant conviction" at the time that Gilbert was indeed speaking the truth.[7] But often in such violent moods Gilbert had bitterly taunted those closest to him; and subsequent events—Gilbert's sober apology, his death in the War, his father's worshipful memory of him—above all Gerald's own diffidence—effectively prevent any follow-up of the story. Further complicating matters is the fact that Gerald, with Dutch courage born of his tension, that very evening first seduces Dollie, Gilbert's wife. He had long been attracted to her, and his scruple against involving her in a situation that might give pain is something that Gilbert mocks him with just before launching into his attack upon his father.

The second scene recalls the day at Melpham when Eorpwald's tomb was actually uncovered. Gerald remembers spraining his ankle immediately upon arrival;

also, his first meeting with Dollie, his hosts the Portways, and other persons of the drama. But except for some slight confusion as to who was with Gilbert at the excavation, he can think of nothing that might substantiate Gilbert's fantastic story.

Part II of the novel tests Gerald's new-found freedom, its opportunities and its limitations. In his professional life he engages in renewed and vigorous activity, not only taking on the editorship of the *History*, but also reviving his work on the Confessor. Before the year is out, however, he realises that it is not too late to settle the unfinished business about Melpham, and that his future happiness absolutely demands that he should do so. After a long and fascinating piece of detective work, he assembles the necessary evidence to prove the truth of Gilbert's story. Significantly, he is able to present his case only at the cost of directly injuring his old friend, Rose Lorimer, who at that point reverts to her former eccentricities, literally with a vengeance. But Gerald has learned that pain is often an inescapable consequence of any moral action, and that now he can accept this.

Gerald learns this truth from a good deal of recently experienced pain inflicted upon him mainly through his association with his family and his involvement in their multifarious activities. Despite his feelings of failed responsibility to his children, and his very real wish to help them out of serious difficulties, he at last recognises that his efforts are useless, or worse than useless: they merely gain him an increased contempt. Accepting this bitter pill of defeat is difficult, and Gerald can do so only with the help of his renewed acquaintance with Dollie. With telling irony, the trail of evidence that ultimately decides the Melpham question leads Gerald back to his former mistress, whom he has deliberately avoided for many years. That he can confront her now is added testimony to his recovered strength. But Gerald meets a different Dollie from the drunken, embittered woman whom he had last seen just before the Second World War. Through the help of Alcoholics Anonymous—which she treats with accustomed but no longer destructive irony—she has permanently cured her dipsomania and has gone on to accept her lot in life with both penetrating insight and a remarkable lack of rancour. The same courage and understanding that help her to face loneliness enable her now to help Gerald to do so. When, aware of the change in Dollie and the hopelessness of his family relationships, he proposes to Dollie that they re-form something of their old alliance, she rejects his suggestion and argues that he really thrives on being on his own. "But you won't leave anything or anybody alone," she tells him. "Look at the way you fuss about your family. You deserve all the raspberries you get from them. And you won't forget the past. Oh! I grant you the Melpham business. That was different. You *had* to act there. But it's over now. You've got to move on."[8]

Entirely able now to accept what he can no longer help, Gerald does move on. To forget the past, and to resume the work on the Confessor that his Melpham investigations had interrupted, he goes at Christmas to Mexico, to the New World—not to the annual family gathering, where he realises he has no place anymore; nor even to Dollie's, despite her invitation, which she is pleased to have him refuse. At the moment of his departure, he accepts from Sir Edgar another new job, that of succeeding him as chairman of the Historical Society. Here as elsewhere Gerald gives earnest of his ability, acquired through hard-won insight and a proper balance of responsibility, to go on living a useful and productive life. Like Dollie, he accepts the conse-quence of his earlier mistakes—loneliness—without the despair that once crippled him; and he begins to form new relationships with people, in a "humanistic way," as Wilson calls it,[9] though precisely what this means only the next novel will clarify. This is the test of Gerald's strength, and of the strength, too, of Wilson's second, but in some ways still unsuccessful novel.

For as a finely organised and fully integrated work of art, the book leaves much wanting. There can be no question that in *Anglo-Saxon Attitudes* Wilson has created a brilliant world of contemporary English life and manners, with a few Continental figures thrown in for added measure. But notwithstanding his wish to demonstrate the Proustian thesis that "the strangest and most unlikely lives are in fact interdependent,"[10] he introduces far more material than he successfully handles or than he requires for the working out of his major themes. Less than a quarter of the way through the book we are aware of an intricate mesh of interrelationships among the characters; and it is chiefly owing to their swift, dramatic presentation that the novel does not swell to twice its size. Perhaps it should; for in this most Dickensian novel the wide range of "attitudes"—Anglo-Saxon and otherwise—crowd together too closely, resulting in a serious blurring of the main focus.[11] Too many influences seem to be at work here—Waugh, Lewis Carroll, Galsworthy, E. M. Forster—in addition to those of Proust and Dickens. At the same time, the greater control of plot and character subordination in comparison with *Hemlock and After* shows some advances in Wilson's development as a novelist. But though they qualify, they do not reverse the main criticism that the "multiplied worlds" of this novel discover more that is ingenious in the author than is satisfying to the reader.

The point becomes clearer with illustrations, through which we may see other techniques Wilson uses. In Part I, Chapter Three, several characters appear who sooner or later contribute to the unravelling of the Melpham mystery. They are Frank Rammage, Lilian Portway, and her granddaughter, Elvira Portway. But clearly these characters are not introduced merely for the sake of solving Gerald's professional riddle. Each of them helps to develop the idea of "philanthropy" that masks the petty tyrannies of many other similarly self-deceived characters in the book. For example, Frank Rammage's benevolence towards the down-and-outers who lodge in his boarding house is only a more ludicrous variation of the patronage that Gerald's older son, Robin, tries to dole out as a director in the family business. Elvira's maternalistic concern for John Middleton's personal career (she is his secretary) is a reflexion, however pale, of Ingeborg's control over all three of her children's affairs. In this fashion, Wilson links together many disparate episodes and, by focusing upon their aspect of self-deception, relates them to one of the book's central themes; yet neither the principle of local thematic unity, nor that of contiguous "Proustian" worlds, is sufficient to counteract what appears to be a surplus of characters and situations in the novel. For all that Lilian Portway and her companion Stephanie Houdet contribute to an already imposing array of parallel situations—Mme Houdet and her son Yves represent the third mother-son situation, Lilian and Elvira one of about a dozen other filial relationships—and for all that the great Mrs Portway reveals of the decadent world of Gerald's young manhood or the present decay of her Merano existence, none of these things has any *essential* place in the novel. Again, the episodes that concern Gerald's former housekeeper, Mrs Salad, may show something of his past life with Dollie and may symbolise at the end the impossibility of resuming that life: but the point is well enough made without her appearance, and the book does not otherwise require her to demonstrate Gerald's humanity. Add to these episodes those that include her grandson, Vin Salad, or that somehow involve Gerald in the homosexual life of his son John, and complications unduly multiply.

That Wilson became aware of this problem in his

novel is evident from his article called "Diversity and Depth," which appeared in a special supplement on the modern English novel in *The Times Literary Supplement*, 15 Aug. 1958. Choosing for his point of departure the "adult" novel set in a framework of social responsibility, as exemplified by the work of George Eliot, Thackeray, and others, he criticises the experimental novel of the early part of our century for its lack of seriousness and the contemporary novel for its lack of depth, even though the latter seems to have restored some of the social setting and other paraphernalia of Victorian fiction. "To combine depth with breadth seems to me the principal problem that must preoccupy the contemporary English novelist," he says.[12] The date of the article is significant, for it suggests that this was the very problem on his mind when he wrote his third novel, *The Middle Age of Mrs Eliot*, also published in 1958. This book again tells the story of Bernard Sands and Gerald Middleton, but with greater moral and artistic success than anything Wilson had up to then achieved.

REFERENCES

1. *W.W.*, p. 260.
2. Cp. Cox, *op. cit.*, p. 237.
3. *W.W.*, p. 261.
4. *A.S.A.*, p. 6.
5. *A.S.A.*, p. 5.
6. *W.W.*, pp. 257-8.
7. *A.S.A.*, p. 168.
8. *A.S.A.*, p. 389.
9. *W.W.*, p. 261.
10. *W.W.*, p. 258.
11. Cp. Scott-Kilvert, *op. cit.*, pp. 49 f.
12. *Op. cit.*, p. viii.

CHAPTER V

THE MIDDLE AGE OF MRS ELIOT

The Middle Age of Mrs Eliot combines the patterns of *Hemlock and After* and *Anglo-Saxon Attitudes*, and adds a significant strengthening of narrative technique. Through two contrasting protagonists, Meg Eliot and her brother, David Parker, Wilson investigates with renewed vigour the possibilities of reconstruction after insight in his most sustained use of plot and sub-plot. At the same time, in the study of David he examines an intellectual humanism that is less disastrous, if much more limited, than the humanism of Bernard Sands. Within this basic structure a number of minor sub-plots also appears to suggest further diversity, but Wilson nowhere allows them to detract seriously from his deeper focus upon the central characters.

Book One of this somewhat Hegelian, three-part novel at once presents Meg Eliot as chairman of the Committee for Aid to the Elderly, a private charity, and proceeds through a series of scenes to dramatise the main interests of her life: her home, friends, fine china, books, entertaining, and—above all—her marriage. The method of exposition is by now familiar; so is Meg, whose character has been lightly traced in the short stories (as Claire, for example, in "Sister Superior") and in the exotic intrusions of Clarissa Crane in *Anglo-Saxon Attitudes*. The very first sentence gives the main bent of her personality: "Meg Eliot was well aware that in taking her place as Chairman of the Committee for the third time in succession she was acting in an unconstitutional way." This self-awareness, we recognise, is the hallmark of the Wilsonian hero: but as we have also seen, it is not in itself proof against deeper self-deception. Despite her tendency towards self-mockery and her self-consciousness about her wealth, smartness, and other external manifestations of her position, which so often allow her to dominate people, Meg is radically deceived about the quality of her success, chiefly because her view of it has not, as yet, been seriously challenged. She is not without some premonitions of a deep-seated threat to her self-esteem—for instance, when she glimpses herself obversely not as an "exotic crane in flight" but "more like some greedy, pecking stork"[1]—but she is able to rationalise these premonitions as "superstitious fear of hubris" that must, through distraction, be disposed of. Her rationalisation resembles Bernard Sands's tendency early in *Hemlock and After*; in the same way, her "constant, hard-working eagerness to fill life with use and pleasure"[2] recalls his belief that "to let life bore you" is the cardinal sin.[3] That her life, much more than Bernard's, is really empty, even vicious, Meg discovers through the intervention of what is ambiguously presented as pure chance, or luck, and a logical consequence of her mode of living: the "spontaneous" sacrifice of her husband to an assassin's bullet. In this way Wilson injects for the first time in his novels an element of metaphysics whose implications he carefully, if not fully, explores.

The death of Bill Eliot, Meg's husband, occurs at Srem Panh airport during their trip around the world. Meg looks forward to this business-and-pleasure trip with divided feelings, for she fears change, the unknown, and is in any case content with her sheltered London existence. Her fear of the unknown is rendered symbolically by her reaction to flying over a desert. Gradually, the barrenness of the landscape takes possession of her imagination: "she found herself lost in it, completely and absolutely bereft of all that made sense of her life,

forsaken and ready for annihilation."[4] The vast empti-
ness, the meaningless plateaux and deceptive saltpans
promising water, are fit emblems for Meg, and her
vision of them shows how much she will have to learn.
Knowledge of how seriously she has underestimated
the effect of her childlessness upon Bill comes to her,
for example, only moments before his death. Her failure
to throw off the desert's grip through customary dis-
tractions—idle conversation, "passionate curiosity," or
reading—further dramatises her readiness for annihilation. She has an uncomfortable moment in which she
feels cut off from her husband and so from all humanity;
for despite her many "social" activities, her only true
communion is with him. When the unknown strikes at
Srem Panh, she is indeed cut off—hurled with a single
blow into the desert she has found so terrifying.

It is typical of both Meg's will and her intelligence
that after the first shock of her experience she can
readily formulate her problem. She sees an almost
childish innocence (a type of evasion, she now realises)
underlying her sophistication and plans a reconstruction
for herself that will better educate her in the ways of the
world and her position in it. On the other hand, she
fears the loss of personal identity as a major threat to her
existence after her husband's death, which because of
their chaotic finances leaves her relatively poor. And
she must somehow come to terms with her sense of guilt
for not providing Bill with the kind of life that would
have brought him happiness rather than a desperate
success—a success (as she puts it) which she drove him
to and then fed upon. These are, in different forms,
basically the same problems that confronted Bernard
Sands and Gerald Middleton: the displacement of
values, the peril to self-identity through undeception,
the burden of guilt for failing in close personal relationships, the search for the right reasons to motivate the
right deeds. That Meg can overcome her problems is

the final tribute, but that victory involves reshaping her character under the discipline of loneliness and self-acceptance is tribute to Wilson's maturing vision as a novelist. For, as in *Anglo-Saxon Attitudes*, insight is not in itself a final goal. In *The Middle Age of Mrs Eliot*, Meg must undergo a series of encounters that will probe, far more deeply than Gerald Middleton's, her ability to live within the limitations of this world and, in particular, within the still narrower limitations of her own being.

Meg's first attempts to confront her predicament with "intelligent realism" stem from premature assertions of independence and pride, and as such they fail badly. The hope of converting her hobby of collecting fine china into some professional use—a hope so precious as to be only half-confessed—is abruptly quashed by Miss Gorres, the woman who had formerly sold her her china and who now enlightens Meg on her amateurishness. When Mr Darlington, the secretary of "Aid to the Elderly," discourages her from seeking social work as a profession, she suffers a second important setback to her self-esteem and her will. She has bravely renounced the easy ways out of her financial predicament—accepting loans or renting part of her house; she wishes instead to emerge from her sheltered life, to "fill the desert inside" her, by becoming "an employed person in a largely employed world."[5] Now she finds herself unexpectedly baffled, even though she recognises that the "lessons in limitation" originating in Srem Panh will inevitably continue in England.[6]

Mr Darlington's rejection is the more baffling to her because he takes the occasion offered him to lay bare the essence of Meg's nature and the way it operates in the world of others. Accurately, almost ruthlessly, he sets before her an image of herself as a woman intensely interested in people of all sorts, but despite her interest, understanding, and charm, unfit to do the main job of helping others to help themselves. She would fail in her

plan, he suggests, because the insight and responsibility
demanded of the social worker are precisely not those
of the society hostess. More profoundly, he exposes Meg's
basic self-centredness, her inability to recognise and to
satisfy the needs of others except as they may also
satisfy her own need to be brilliant.[7] After a period of
retreat, and weeks of nightmares, Meg awakens to a
new plan and enters the Garsington Secretarial College.

Directly contrasting with Meg's activist approach to
her problems is the position taken by her brother, David,
as he confronts his own. An extreme pacifist, who does
not confine his attitude to physical non-violence, he
believes in self-discipline worked out in a life of daily
"Martha tasks" that has enabled him and his partner,
Gordon Paget, to build up a successful nursery-garden
called Andredaswood in the South Downs. He is a
kind of humanist also, but is wary of the looseness and
evasiveness of the term and recognises at the outset, as
Bernard Sands did not, the harm that is latent in all
human relationships, even in the assertion of love.
Reluctant to hurt, he thus follows a path of carefully
measured withdrawal and self-effacement, maintaining
that the world presently requires "a simmering down
of personality, of human achievement too . . . in order
that we may start up again."[8] In his views he has been
deeply influenced by Gordon, a believing Christian:
but David is determined to fuse his friend's way of life
with his own agnosticism.[9] A more profound difference
between David and his sister cannot be imagined, and in
fact they have in their adult life grown strangers to one
another.

When Gordon dies, the victim of a lingering illness,
the contrast between Meg and David intensifies. In his
friend David had found "a love, and the object of his
love [that] had declared, so openly and once for all,
that loneliness was the condition of man, a loneliness to
be endured and fulfilled in the constant disguise of

human contact."[10] If Gordon's illness understandably raises doubts in David about a life of "ordered despair" or the virtues of self-denial, Gordon's dying—the climax of David's life—reaffirms his convictions, for he finds that they enable him to meet this loss "decently for himself and, within the great limitations of human aid, decently for others."[11] David is careful, however, not to congratulate himself on any superior wisdom. It is merely his greater luck, he tells himself, than say Meg's, whose life, unlike his own, seems designed to hide her from the reality of loneliness instead of preparing her to accept it. But once again, as in the account of Bill Eliot's death at Srem Panh, Wilson sidesteps the full implications of what he chooses to call, ambiguously, "luck" or chance in human experience. Through the tactic of self-irony—as habitual to Meg as to other important characters in his fiction—Wilson allows David to fend off the imputation of smugness rather than shoulder the burden of greater wisdom. Moreover, David's agnosticism (or Wilson's) does not allow too close an investigation of such "luck." Be this as it may, David is resolved after Gordon's death to live out his life in both the loneliness and the fulfilment he has accepted. But shortly afterwards, when Meg suffers a complete breakdown and is brought to the nursery-garden to recuperate, his resolve is unexpectedly thwarted.

Meg's breakdown is the result, generally, of her inadequate resistance to the assaults of loneliness. More specifically, it stems from her failure to adjust satisfactorily to the lives of friends who, with an attitude born of kindred loneliness, take her in. Before the breakdown, her self-imposed discipline of study and frugality, centring upon her determination to pass the secretarial course, is a precursor of future peace. It almost approaches David's view of an "ordered despair,"[12] but Meg is not yet strong enough to withstand the need she feels for other fulfilment. She therefore turns to her friends, the same ones whom before her widowhood she had referred to as her "lame ducks," partly because— no longer married themselves—they could not fly with the rest of her smart social set. Now that she is a lame duck herself, searching to know the ways of the world and her place in it, she discovers (ironically) that they are the ones who educate her most thoroughly. And most painfully: for the lessons in limitation that they teach are the limitations of friendship.

Meg's failures with her friends are the result of exactly the reasons set forth by Mr Darlington: she charms her way into their fixed patterns of life and then (like Gerald Middleton) commits well-intentioned blunders trying to solve their problems—problems which she does not understand and which, anyway, cannot be remedied through outside interference. Meanwhile, on her part, she cannot accept the ways of life that they hold out to her. She rejects out of hand the life of a "down the drain lady" with its superficial attraction of "punch-drunk bliss" that Poll, a divorcée, tries to recommend.[13] She is equally averse to any other form of "plucky death in life"—either the calculated early remarriage that Lady Pirie urges, or the isolation of Jill Stokes's frozen affections. At the same time, she is fully aware of the sacrifice in friendship that these rejections will cost. Deeply troubled by such setbacks in her personal relationships, as well as by her inability to help David in his moment of grief, Meg finds that passing the secretarial course, on which she has worked so hard, cannot head off a serious emotional collapse.

At Andredaswood, recovering from her breakdown, Meg begins by overcompensating: her initial adjustment is a pathetic attempt to accommodate herself to every- one and everything. Only with the appearance of her former bite and humour does she begin to emerge from the cocoon of her neurosis. But as she reassumes her old identity as a charming, witty, and thoroughly attractive person, she finds that she is again apt to impose herself upon others, this time more subtly and deceptively. Gradually, she lures David away from his Martha tasks into sharing her diversions. She presses him to re-activate things, like the amateur string quartet and his doctorial dissertation, that as gestures of "indifferentism" he has deliberately let go to seed. She encourages resumption of the nursery-garden's biannual cocktail parties, and then fills Gordon's place as their star.

Just as David falls further and further into the trap of cosiness and sentimental devotion that his sister has unwittingly laid for him, Meg suddenly awakes and leaves Andredaswood. But her awakening is not truly abrupt: the whole of her recent experience, including the recovery we have been observing, has prepared her for this step. Like Bernard Sands, she at length perceives the danger of this "last temptation" and can resist. When David pleads with her to remain, her reply deepens and clarifies Dollie's renunciation of Gerald Middleton in *Anglo-Saxon Attitudes*, or Terence Lambert's of Elizabeth in *Hemlock and After*. She reminds David that his loneliness is his strength, and she will not destroy it. Nor will she destroy herself by conforming to a life of abnegation and withdrawal to which she is unsuited. The only way that she can be of use, she recognises, is to be with people and to keep her curiosity. She does not deny David's truth; it simply is not hers. "I'm quite a silly person, David, really," she concludes.[14]

Meg, of course, is not a silly person. She has faced up to the limitations of her nature and, given both insight and experience enough for it to mature, she is ready to take her chances in the world. Unlike Bernard, she refuses to allow the defects in her character or the inevitable complexities of human motive to overwhelm her. Instead, she wisely relies upon her virtues—the same charm and curiosity and desire to be useful of her earlier life—tempered now by her knowledge of their

E

true value for herself and for others. If she sees that her
life must still be essentially lonely, she sees too that she
can find some measure of self-fulfilment, and live. David,
in his quite different mode of existence, will also continue living: the pain that his sister's parting causes him
is just retribution for his temporary lapse from principles
that once more appear vindicated. Seeing more profoundly, perhaps, than Meg into the limitations of the
world, he demonstrates that his withdrawal does not
deny life, but, paradoxically, affirms it. Wilson thus
presents two kinds of heroism, both admittedly limited,
but neither of them pessimistic or cynical. They are, as
he elsewhere suggests, the only ones available to us.[15]

If a third kind exists, it is shown by Gordon who,
more than any other character in Wilson's fiction, face
from the outset "the dual nature of all human action."[1]
By accepting both good and evil in the human heart, h
is able to help and to hurt others, even in the deepe:
personal relationships (consider, for example, his sexu
promiscuity and its effect upon David). His insight ir
Meg's predicament when David first goes to meet l
leads up to a signal act of heroism—his acceptance
death and an attempt to comfort his friend. The
episodes in the last weeks of his life in which Gord
falls beneath his own standards of behaviour do i
alter his stature as a magnificent human being; if ar
thing, they reassert it.[17] But though Gordon's life—ar
his love of it—make David's modified monasticism lo
pale and Meg's career trivial, Wilson is reluctant t
explore the religious faith that underlies these advan
tages. This reluctance is unfortunate, for in Gordon we
catch sight of other possibilities for humanism in the
modern world—a religious humanism—which might, if
tested, provide a richer yield than the secular humanism
Wilson has cultivated and, it seems, fairly exhausted
However, pious frauds like Edie in "Union Reunion"
or Dr Early, the "Christian humanist" in "Learning's

Little Tribute," far outnumber the truly religious characters in Wilson's fiction. Moreover, since Wilson is himself a confirmed atheist, and since in his fourth novel, *The Old Men at the Zoo*, Dr Charles Langley-Beard is the most mercilessly pilloried of all his religious hypocrites, it is not likely that he will soon try the different approach to humanism that Gordon suggests.

The technical developments of the novel, on the other hand, are more promising and recall the concluding remarks of "Diversity and Depth." There Wilson had said that to strike the right balance between breadth of vision and depth of focus, writers must continue to concern themselves with "the viewpoint of narration and a re-examination of the interior monologue form to see how its artificiality can be more happily combined with the direct effects of dialogue and action."[18] In *The Middle Age of Mrs Eliot* we can see the results of his own preoccupation with these matters. Despite the inherent difficulty of the task, his handling of contrasting points of view is successful until almost the very end, where a serious and unnecessary reversal of emphasis seems to occur. During the first two parts of the book (up to Meg's breakdown), the main focus rests, as it should, upon the principal character and her experiences. At the same time, the sub-plot maintains a remarkably intense emphasis of its own without in any way detracting from the point of view that it is designed to complement. But when in Book Three the actions of both plots coalesce, Wilson shifts the emphasis of viewpoint mainly to David. It is true that Meg's breakdown may at first lend itself more readily to observances of her rather than by her; and it is also true that except for her recovery the action of the main plot is essentially complete, while the testing of David—his temptation and fall—is yet to come. But a shift of this kind two-thirds through a novel is always dangerous and at best awkward. Recalling Wilson's skill in presenting the first meeting between

David and Meg, and his successful handling there of both points of view simultaneously, we may question the need of a shift at all. The emphasis of Book Three may be intended to balance the corresponding emphasis of Book One, where David scarcely appears: but aesthetic satisfaction through symmetry of this type cannot be seriously argued. In any event, the rapid conclusion of the novel once again shows Meg in the ascendant as she describes through her letters to David the various jobs she has held as a private secretary. The intrinsic equilibrium of the novel thus seems to insist upon preserving the original relative emphases. But however we judge upon this point, it is certain that for the first time in his novels Wilson nowhere permits any other alternative points of view, not even Gordon Paget's, to blur his main foci. An impressive number of minor and secondary characters appear, as usual: but since he does not preface this book with a listing of the *dramatis personae*, Wilson himself may have recognised how successfully he has kept all of his characters to their appropriate and carefully defined tasks in developing the major themes of his book.

It is harder to see—certainly it would be harder to illustrate—a collateral advance in Wilson's use of the interior monologue, except to say that it appears in this more deeply probing novel more often and more extensively than in his earlier works. He retains the mixed form of the monologue as in the short stories, which seems to combine happily indeed with the more direct effects of dialogue and action.[19] Significantly, in *The Middle Age of Mrs Eliot* there is no detective hunt such as Gerald Middleton was forced to undertake: the action is far more completely internalised as Meg sets out to fill "the desert within."

Wilson's increased adeptness in the use of interior monologue enables him also to recount much of the past history of his characters as and when it becomes most useful or appropriate to do so. Meg's and David's early life—for instance, their recollections of growing up together, or of their mother—is thus naturally presented. There is no recourse to the technically disingenuous device of Gerald's prolonged and artificially controlled reverie at the end of Part One of *Anglo-Saxon Attitudes*. This new facility, of course, may be seen as something originally developed in the short stories. Nevertheless, with proportionally so much more material to synthesise in a novel, Wilson has here registered some important gains.

In what is the best short survey of Wilson's work to date, Mr Ian Scott-Kilvert gives a succinct and perceptive statement concerning the technical achievements of *The Middle Age of Mrs Eliot* as compared to the earlier novels. Where once the short story technique was everywhere apparent, especially in "the speed of narration and the habit of presenting a series of situations rather than developing them," Wilson has here discovered how to give his subject the "more leisurely, muted treatment" it requires.[20] And if we add that in the process of perfecting his remarkable narrative technique Wilson has also clarified and strengthened his moral vision, then he is another of those writers who illustrate an important facet of modern critical theory—that the essential fusion of great form with great matter is the basis for truly distinguished literary accomplishment.

REFERENCES

1. *Mrs Eliot*, p. 38.
2. *Ibid.*
3. *H.A.*, p. 56.
4. *Mrs Eliot*, p. 79.
5. *Mrs Eliot*, p. 169.
6. *Mrs Eliot*, p. 188.
7. *Mrs Eliot*, p. 196.
8. *Mrs Eliot*, p. 290.
9. Cp. E. M. Forster's call for "apathy, uninventiveness, and inertia," in "Art for Art's sake," *Two Cheers for Democracy*, 1951.
10. *Mrs Eliot*, pp. 202 f.
11. *Mrs Eliot*, p. 202.
12. See *Mrs Eliot*, p. 221.
13. *Mrs Eliot*, p. 273.
14. *Mrs Eliot*, p. 426.
15. *W.W.*, p. 261.
16. *H.A.*, p. 146.
17. *Mrs Eliot*, pp. 204–14.
18. *T.L.S.*, 15 Aug. 1958, p. viii.
19. See, *e.g.*, *Mrs Eliot*, p. 278.
20. Scott-Kilvert, *op. cit.*, p. 50.

CHAPTER VI

A BIT OFF THE MAP

In the creative life of a truly developing writer, every work is a transitional work, an attempt to push forward the boundaries of his experience and the understanding of his art. Wilson's first three novels show this continuing development in both their moral quest and artistic competence. Part of the continuity must be traced, however, through *A Bit Off the Map*, a collection of stories published between the second and third novels, but a book whose significance as transitional work emerges most clearly when it is taken out of chronological sequence.

First, the obvious connexions with earlier work. Probably most fiction writers share Wilson's admittedly paternalistic attitude towards his characters—though not, perhaps, to the extent of reintroducing a "leftover" character, like Elizabeth Sands, at the end of a subsequent novel.[1] Often they feel compelled to re-examine such characters in a new disguise or slightly different pattern of events. The American novelist and short story writer, Herbert Gold, has said that a concern of this sort may even transform intended short stories into longer works.[2] As we have seen, the principal characters of Wilson's first three novels have important, basic family resemblances to each other, as well as to more lightly sketched characters in the short stories. This kind of resemblance appears also between one of the minor characters in *Anglo-Saxon Attitudes*, Timothy Middleton, and the main character of "After the Show," one of three *novella* in *A Bit Off the Map*. In Robin and Marie Hélène's son, Wilson very likely saw possibilities for

developing both the character of the young, middle-class
intellectual and the situation in which he comes to the
aid of his father's hysterical, party-crashing mistress,
Elvira Portway. Wilson doubtless saw, too, how he
could develop the general problem of Ibsen's *The Wild
Duck* in a comic or satiric mode instead of a tragic one;
for it is no accident that this story opens with Maurice
Liebig returning with his grandmother from a performance
of that play. Maurice is not exactly a Gregers Werle, and
the person he sets out to "save" is no Hedvig Ekdal.
But his longing for "a proper life of high responsibility, of
tempered adult courage" and his disdain for "this age
of mediocrity, of grubbing merchants and sordid arti-
sans"[3] have enough of the Messianic spirit of Gregers'
"claims of the ideal." Maurice's adventure in collecting
such a claim, however, does not end with a young girl's
suicide—it begins with one, or rather with the comic,
abortive attempt of his uncle's mistress to kill herself
with an overdose of aspirin.

The more searching themes of this story, on the other
hand, deal with certain qualities that Maurice shares
with Timothy Middleton and many other teenagers of
their class and breeding: priggishness, a smugly critical
attitude towards his elders, and a rather callow seriousness. Through such aspects of his character Wilson
develops in great detail the conflict of generations that is
a *leit-motif* in much of his fiction and that becomes
dominant in his play, *The Mulberry Bush*, and in *The Old
Men at the Zoo*. For Maurice, like Timothy, typifies the
generation immediately following that of James and
Sonia Sands (either of the boys might be their son,
grown older by a dozen years). Still in reaction to the
liberalism of the nineteen-thirties, he is somewhat suspicious, too, of the neo-Victorianism of his forebears.
Hence, his point of view is fairly complex, and, aided
by his self-consciousness and faltering confidence, it
compels sympathy. In brief, Maurice dramatises the

basic antagonisms that inevitably arise between young men and those responsible for "a world they never made," but particularly at a time of rapid transition, when it becomes harder than ever for young people to rebel in the name of some clear-cut ideal.

The conflict of generations, the plight of inspired youth, likewise appears as a major theme in the title story, "A Bit Off the Map." Incorporating pungent satire of Teddy boys, beatniks, and others of both the older and younger generations, Wilson writes an allegory of post-war England trying to find itself amidst the din of discordant, prophetic voices and conflicting loyalties. The central character, Kennie Martin, is a twenty-one year-old psychopath who is desperately searching for "The Truth" and hopes that by consorting with "The Crowd," a group of left-wing writers and their girl friends, he will discover it. His eventual— and disastrous—disillusionment develops through the exposure of characters like Huggett, an anti-rationalist poet, and Reg, a pseudo-Laurentian novelist. (Except for a few asides in *Hemlock and After* and *Anglo-Saxon Attitudes*,[4] or the stylistic parodies at the end of *For Whom the Cloche Tolls*, such literary satire is unprecedented in Wilson's fiction, and never so sustained as here.) Kennie's despair touches the heart of seventy-four year-old Colonel Lambourn, who tries to console him. But the colonel turns out to be a paranoiac, far more off balance than even Kennie. Convinced that by the juxtaposition of a series of maps of the realm he has discovered the location of England's greatest treasure, he suffers acutely from frustrations brought on by constant, official rebuff. Thus when he disarmingly provokes Kennie into confessing his own quest, the colonel's well-worn routine automatically clicks on, but with dire consequences. In no mood to be duped once more, Kennie sees red, bludgeons the old man, and runs off leaving him, presumably, to die.

Apart from these shifts in the objects or mode of satire, a greater difference exists between "A Bit Off the Map" and "After the Show," one which has to do with the technique of presenting a complex point of view. In his earlier stories, Wilson registers ambivalence towards his characters by showing them as alternately selfish and kind, troubled and aloof, or in other ways repulsive and sympathetic. In the present collection, he tries to show the ambivalence that his characters feel *towards themselves*. He does this, moreover, without resorting to mere character sketches in which the narrative aspects of the short story tend to disappear. This attempt to internalise conflict is of course part of Wilson's ambition since *Anglo-Saxon Attitudes* and derives as well from his experience, not entirely successful, of rendering ambivalence in *Hemlock and After*.

"A Bit Off the Map" fails, on the whole, to achieve this deeper focus. Because of its experimental nature, it is none the less interesting. Here Wilson tries more forthrightly than, say, in "Necessity's Child" to mix a first- and third-person narration, beginning with Kennie's long monologue and switching over, when The Crowd appears on the scene, to conventional third-person techniques. The reason for this switch is not merely to provide a comic climax for the story in the impromptu party that The Crowd foists upon Clara Turnbull-Henderson, a hostess of literary leanings. More importantly, Wilson's intention is to present an exterior view of the action and theme as well as the interior one provided by Kennie. Complicating matters and somewhat deepening the allegory of Kennie and his madness is The Crowd's continuing debate upon the qualities of the man of Heroic Will, a figure concocted out of Huggett's theories and incorporated by Reg in his novel. But madness, or at any rate such confusion as emanates from Kennie's feeble-minded questing, is hardly the best vehicle for rendering subjective ambivalence. And

Wilson's allegorical structure creaks so loudly at times that the subtleties psychologically most appropriate to ambivalence are quite obliterated. Kennie's struggle after The Truth and his longing to find himself in it are far better realised in "After the Show," where The Truth becomes a lower case affair, involving Maurice in a set of conflicting attitudes towards himself and others to which we can much better respond.

In "More Friend Than Lodger," another *novella*, Wilson sustains the first-person narrator throughout the story but again does not fully capture the attitude of deeply felt ambivalence. It is quite likely that this story, in contrast to the others, depends upon just such a lack of real inner conflict for the basis of its comedy. June Raven, the narrator and principal character, is a young married woman of about twenty-six or -seven who is convinced that she can have her cake and eat it, if only she keeps her eye upon her object and does not let sentimentality become an obstructive influence. For June, having her cake and eating it means retaining her secure social position while indulging in more social "adventures" than her position would ordinarily permit.[5] Wilfulness, self-assurance, and whimsy surely connect her to Meg Eliot as we first know her, but Mrs Raven is more incorrigibly a predator (as her name suggests) than Mrs Eliot ever seems; and much less profound—if for that reason perhaps more amusing. Though she is quite aware that most people are "a mass of contradictions," and that her attitude towards them is (consequently or not) "ambiguous,"[6] she does not allow herself to be seriously troubled by these insights any more than she is by her own contradictory wishes—for the reasons already given. In a sense, we have here the personality but not the character or moral point of view that are essential to the development of Wilson's later heroine. As the story of an a-moral woman in search of hedonism without insecurity, "More Friend than Lodger" is an ironic, comic commentary upon the perplexities of ambivalent attitudes. But—June's headaches and tempers notwithstanding—the story cannot pretend to a very great deal more.

True ambivalence, seriously rendered, is to be found rather in two short and quite similar stories, whose titles fairly proclaim their theme. They are "Once a Lady" and "Higher Standards." In both stories the chief characters are women whose conflicts derive from a deeply divided attitude towards themselves and towards their chosen lot in life. Elsie Corfe in "Higher Standards" is a young village school teacher who because of superior intellectual pretensions finds herself cut off from young men with whom she might otherwise have normal social contact. Living with her spiteful and gossipy mother and invalid father accentuates Elsie's emotional starvation. It threatens, furthermore, to rob her of what small satisfaction she gets from maintaining her intellectual superiority (underlined by her having to teach the "Standard IV's"). Unlike June Raven, neither her personality nor her circumstances allow Elsie to have her cake *or* eat it; on the contrary, she appears almost immobilised between these alternatives.

Esther Barrington in "Once a Lady" likewise finds it impossible to satisfy incompatible desires. Ostracised by her family and social class because of her marriage, she leads a backbreaking life as a Midlands village shopkeeper. Only the tenderness she feels towards Jim, her husband, keeps her going. When the dreariness of her lot undermines even that recompense for all her sacrifices, she begins to long for the comforts and security of her earlier existence. Through her friendship with Eileen Carter, she tries to reassert her old identity, but is soon disillusioned. The comfort she would find at Eileen's house has its price and demands its own sacrifice from the slim store of self-respect and wifely devotion that Esther struggles to maintain. Thus both Elsie and

Esther anticipate Meg Eliot's predicament. In a world hostile or at best indifferent to their wishes, they try by sheer act of will to preserve some part of their personal identity or integrity. And the little that they would preserve appears ironically to be far too much.

In other ways besides the presentation of ambivalence Wilson attempts to subdue his tone and deepen his perspective in *A Bit Off the Map*, without at the same time surrendering his customary force. One means is through deliberate anti-climax. It is not altogether a new technique, for several of his earlier stories, like "Et Dona Ferentes" and "A Little Companion," have such endings. But in contrast to the final shock upon which many of the earlier stories depend for their effect, most of these try to mitigate the impact of violence (psychological or physical) by something less sensational and more deeply moving. Consider, for example, "A Flat Country Christmas" (first published in 1950 as "Old, Old Message"). As ambitious but overworked and overtense Ray Slater participates in a party game at Christmas with his wife and another couple, he brings the whole movement of the story to a climax when he gazes into the mirror in which each one by turns has pretended to see his future. Tears streaming down his face, Ray suddenly exclaims, "Oh! My God! I've seen Nothing!"[7] The story might well have ended here, or, as in "Rex Imperator," with a final paragraph describing how the victim's wife sympathetically and successfully takes charge of a disintegrating situation. Instead, the shock of violence is transmuted to something else. Ray's wife is unable to restore order; neither are the other couple, their hosts. Harshly sweeping aside their expressions of concern, Ray himself concludes the episode. Suddenly shifting his mood again, he says, "I'm sorry. . . . It's not of any importance," and stares into the fire.[8]

In "A Sad Fall," anti-climax is similarly employed to convey resignation and other attitudes in the face of despair. Near the end of the Second World War John Appleby visits the crumbling country home of an old school friend and finds that his friend's aged mother, Mrs Tanner, is living alone with a thirteen year-old boy named Roger, the last of the evacuees, whose parents apparently do not want him back. Roger is a "sensible and ordinary" boy, in John's opinion,[9] hardly brilliant or talented, but none the less worth taking pains with as a sensitive human being. Moreover, John quickly sees that the underlying misery of the boy's life owes much to the selfishness of his patroness and her blind egocentricity. When, in order to compete with her for their visitor's attentions, Roger plays "spy" and falls off a roof, John shocks Mrs Tanner by bluntly rejecting her sentimental cant about never forgiving herself if the boy dies.

If the impact of violence were all that was wanted, the story might have ended with Roger's fall, or with the psychological violence of the subsequent dialogue. But the old woman's reaction also interests Wilson. After John, like Ray Slater, savagely turns upon his hostess, he then dully apologises. "I'm sorry," he says; "if the remark upset you, please think I said it to help or anything else you like."[10] Realising that she will now be alone with John in the house, Mrs Tanner panics and decides to accompany the ambulance to the hospital. When her hysteria dies down, she reassures herself that her fears are "entirely irrational," but fails nevertheless to comprehend the enormity of what has happened or of her part in bringing it to pass.

"Ten Minutes to Twelve," the last story in the volume, will recall some of our original observations. The time is New Year's Eve 1956, and the setting resembles the Middletons' Christmas gathering in *Anglo-Saxon Attitudes*. Three generations and several points of view are represented: Lord Peacehaven, a rich old magnate gone mad, and his wife; their older son, Walter, who has stayed in the family business; his wife, Diana, and their children, Geoff and Patience; and Roland, the Peacehaven's younger son, a scientist. Far from having a conventional plot, the story revolves around various attitudes to the changing times, particularly to the age of "rugged individualism" represented by Lord Peacehaven. Walter and Roland, reflecting the sibling rivalry of Robin and John Middleton, use their contrasting professional competences to express a mutual hostility: but neither seems much concerned about his father. Geoff and Patience, on the other hand, as serious, uncompromising adolescents with conflicting authoritarian and liberalist convictions, disagree violently about their grandfather. His strange, megalomaniacal New Year's memorandum, calling for UNITY and ACTION, precipitates their quarrel. Only Lady Peacehaven remains detached, able to settle back with her husband to a life of the past. When Geoff finally is sent into the garden to bring in the New Year luck, genteel Nurse Carver, one of the company present, completes the political and social allegory by commenting: "He's the spit image of Lord Peacehaven, isn't he? ... perhaps *he'll* grow up to be quite a great man."[11]

Directly inspired by the Suez crisis in 1956, the action of "Ten Minutes to Twelve" is, however, almost completely externalised in the manner of Wilson's earlier stories, except for the long memorandum which begins the piece and is a variant form of Kennie Martin's opening monologue. As the last story in the book, it complements the first one. "A Bit Off the Map" ends with the enraged young man assaulting Colonel Lambourn, a contemporary of Lord Peacehaven's and like him, mad. In "Ten Minutes to Twelve," Geoff defends his grandfather, does not think him mad at all, and promises to become a similar force in his own time. But for someone who has lived through the period 1918–1941, both threats are equally sinister. Kennie and Geoff are thus far less ambiguous figures than Maurice Liebig, who somewhat shares their dissatisfactions and longing, but retains the saving grace of less extreme self-assurance or doubt. The social and political implications of all these stories, as well as Wilson's play, *The Mulberry Bush*, are more fully examined later on in *The Old Men at the Zoo*, his fourth novel, where the underlying human problems are likewise more profoundly scrutinised.

REFERENCES

1. *W.W.*, p. 263; *A.S.A.*, p. 393.
2. *Fifteen by Three*, New York 1957, pp. 104 f.
3. *B.O.M.*, p. 114.
4. *H.A.*, p. 14; *A.S.A.*, p. 62.
5. *B.O.M.*, p. 54.
6. *B.O.M.*, pp. 60, 58.
7. *B.O.M.*, p. 47.
8. *B.O.M.*, p. 48.
9. *B.O.M.*, p. 161.
10. *B.O.M.*, p. 173.
11. *B.O.M.*, p. 193.

CHAPTER VII

PLAYS

It was only to be expected that, given his histrionic sensibility, Wilson should turn early in his career to writing plays. *The Mulberry Bush*, his first one, was originally produced by the Bristol Old Vic on 27 Sep. 1955. Later, in revised form, it was chosen to inaugurate the repertory of the English Stage Company, and began its run at the Royal Court Theatre, London, on 2 Apr. 1956. The play was not entirely successful in either of these productions, and was withdrawn from the London stage on 19 May.[1] Since then Wilson has not had another stage play produced but has written several television scripts. These may represent a compromise between his wish to see his stories on film and the satisfaction of more direct control over his work than the cinema allows.[2] In addition, he has written a radio play, "Skeletons and Assegais," for the B.B.C. Third Programme. This appeared recently in *Transatlantic Review*, but none of the television plays has yet been published.

Chronologically, *The Mulberry Bush* appears just between the first two novels and may explain why *Anglo-Saxon Attitudes*, of all his novels, is the most theatrically conceived. The preoccupation with humanism as a direct and charitable response to individual human beings—as opposed, that is, to a code of behaviour with which to deal with them—once again provides the central theme. Here, however, Wilson develops it by focusing upon the representatives of three generations, as figuratively they dance round the object which gives the play its title.[3] Rose and James Padley, now in their seventies,

F

are still living proponents of an atheist, liberal, activist attitude towards world politics and human affairs that appears distinctly dated. Their closest forebears in Wilson's earlier work are Priscilla and Robin Harker in "Such Darling Dodos," who likewise may owe part of their origin to Sidney and Beatrice Webb. The Padleys' children, Robert (who has just died) and Cora (who may be fatally ill), reflect the weakening of the Padley code in the next generation. Despite his brilliant career as a humanitarian, Robert is found after his death to be someone who missed much human warmth. His apparently happy and satisfactory marriage was in this sense a failure. He therefore felt driven to compensate for it in relationships of adultery, which are made to appear not so much sordid as rather comic and pathetic. Cora, on the other hand, has sought fulfilment in marriage to a rich business man, and now as his widow finds herself materially well off. Her frank devotion to discreet and expensive pleasures is a different but related criticism of the Padley code, as well as the harbinger of other problems that Wilson examines in *The Middle Age of Mrs Eliot*.

The third generation of Padleys is represented by Ann, Robert's daughter, and Simon Fellowes, Cora's son. But here Wilson introduces a number of other characters in order to delineate various contemporary views more completely. For this is, in every sense, a *contemporary* play, particularly as it deals with issues involving the perennial problem of how people must struggle with their past inheritance in order to live in the present and prepare for the future. One approach to the problem is shown through Peter Lord, a young colleague of James Padley at St Roland's College, where both have done historical research and where James has lived for many years as Warden. Peter is a believer in education and has almost decided to take a Government job supervising the teaching of history in schools. In order to do so, however, he must disappoint the Padleys, who want him to spend a year in America with James, now retiring as Warden, and who anyway cannot imagine a protegé of theirs becoming a bureaucrat. Peter's situation is further complicated because he loves Ann and wishes to marry her. That he bids fair to overcome all these obstacles to personal and professional success is a function of his more or less enlightened self-interest, his principles, and his devotion to the people he loves most.

Kurt Landeck is another member of the younger generation who in several ways becomes Peter's foil. A German refugee taken in by the elder Padleys, he has since childhood experienced brutality intimately. While his father, a noted Jewish historian, was being murdered, his Aryan mother obtained a divorce in order to marry a Nazi. As an explanation of Kurt's invidious opportunism—a pathetic attempt to ape the Nietzschian superman—this background information does not succeed: the young man appears much more like a modern reincarnation of the clever slave or parasite from classical comedy and farce. It is largely through his conniving that the hypocrisy under which Robert Padley lived is revealed. Kurt plots throughout the play solely to advance his own interests and, when that fails, takes satisfaction in wounding Rose and James, whose patronising philanthropy he has long resented.

But the centre of interest remains with the youngest generation of Padleys, the grandchildren Ann and Simon. Simon is a study in despair: successful in his career as a barrister, he is a failure as a Padley and, what is more, a man. One gesture of his despair is his unscrupulous and rather puerile sexual adventures, particularly with Wendy Tellick—the neurotic daughter of his former housemaster who, like Kurt, is sheltered by his grandparents. Another is his substitution of the legal code of the courts for his family's moral and humanitarian principles, with which he has become thoroughly disillusioned. Against such behaviour Ann, whom he wishes to marry, struggles to protect herself. It is upon her, silent though she is throughout most of Act I, that the action of the play ultimately focuses—specifically, upon her wish to preserve what is basically sound in the Padleys' heritage—their concern for human values—without any of their self-deceptions.

Peter Lord's role in courting Ann is thus an attempt to reconcile past and present realities in order to build for the future, for he is above all a man of the future. That their union may be possible and then fruitful, he first must see to it that Ann can suffer her illusions about her parents and grandparents to be destroyed without falling into a cynicism comparable to Simon's. The attacks upon her father—and through him, upon the whole Padley tradition—come in the person of Mrs Geraldine Loughton-Moore, Robert's former mistress, and later through Captain Wallcott, who early in Robert's career as a social reformer had been the dupe of one of his sexual indiscretions. Both make essentially the same point about Robert: that he was an emotionally starved human being who had to find in illicit relationships what neither his humanitarian activities nor his wife's intellectual and social companionship—both extensions of highminded Padleyism—could provide. Although after Robert's death the elder Padleys are aware of his mistress's existence, they decide not to enlighten their granddaughter about Geraldine's express wish to see her. Peter objects to this evasiveness, but it is through the malicious offices of Wendy, who shares Kurt's resentment and is anyhow jealous of Ann, that Geraldine is at last brought to St Roland's.

For all her comic affectation, which so distresses the Padleys, Geraldine emerges as a person quite aware of what she is about. She introduces to the surviving members of the family what she had earlier introduced to Robert, something that, superficially, appears as mere impulsiveness or whimsy but that really originates in true feeling. Her special concern is Ann, whose tight control over her emotions Geraldine tries to break down, but only to afford her a means of more direct and sincere response to the people around her. In this way Ann may discover the missing part of her nature that will make her a more complete human being. In another way, Peter seconds Geraldine, and goes further with her to try to enlighten Rose and James. Kurt and Wendy, in their perverse or certainly more selfish fashion, also score against the Padleys, rejecting at last their "good works" along with their patronage.

How successful all these efforts are in effecting a happy conclusion remains ambiguous. Ann finally rejects Simon and agrees to marry Peter, but their future happiness is by no means guaranteed: something in Peter's control over Ann suggests that it may turn out quite differently. James seems to have learned much, but his attempt to share this knowledge with his wife fails, leaving him, as the stage directions indicate, "a broken old man."[4] Rose, discouragingly, appears confident that she is and has been right in her programme of professional good works as well as in her more private devotions. Nevertheless, at the final curtain, she does issue Wendy her marching orders, an act that implies a definite shift from her earlier complacency towards such unfortunate "lame dogs." The attacks upon her by Kurt and (more seriously and less maliciously) by Peter have had their salutary effect, it seems, even if she is unable to bring herself to establish a new and more feeling relationship with her husband. But then again, she may here only be illustrating a logical consequence of James's earlier argument that, however right they may have been in their work, in their family relationships they have utterly failed and must face up to it.[5]

What James says, of course, is almost exactly what Dollie tells Gerald Middleton near the end of *Anglo-Saxon Attitudes*. Gerald, younger by some ten years or

so than Rose, can take it. It may be too late for Rose
Padley, and for all his remonstrating, for James Padley,
too. The point is—and it is borne out in many different
ways throughout the play—that human relationships are
seldom resolved in clear-cut fashion. Where they appear
to be, we are struck by something less than human, as in
Kurt's cold-blooded manipulations. No one else emerges
in the play without quite human admixtures of both
good and evil—the results, often, of either insight or
blindness about themselves and others. That is, Wilson
seems to suggest, what makes them persons, after all,
and what moves us about them, making us at the same
time, through the powers of the imagination, more
fully aware of our own basic humanity.

Despite the seriousness of the theme, the intelligence
of its presentation, and an abundance of verbal wit, *The
Mulberry Bush* was not a great theatrical success. Audrey
Williamson's criticisms of it as "not a warmly human"
play but one that exists on some "detached intellectual
plane," are typical,[6] and Wilson himself has commented
upon its lack of sufficient "theatrical power."[7] To be
sure, the play belongs to an older type of theatre—the
theatre of Ibsen and Shaw—rather than that of Osborne
and Williams. Wilson's play is not without passion:
but the kind that it generates comes from somewhere
within the cranium rather than from the gut, and
this has put off the professionals—theatre critics, who
regard Wilson as a gifted amateur, and doubtless actors,
producers and others as well. Nevertheless, if the frag-
mented contemporary theatre, as Wilson elsewhere
analyses it, is ever going to reconcile the basic demand
of the professional for "dramatic tension" with the intellectual's insistence upon mature representations of
emotion and intelligence, then "it is desirable that someone now and again should speak up for less theatrically
effective plays like 'Danton's Death,' 'Prince Genji,' or
'Who's Your Father?' that on their different levels are,

above all, intelligent."[8] Only through such criticism—
Mary McCarthy's, for example—does Wilson believe
the theatre may eventually avoid degenerating into
either "an arty adolescent charade or a well-trimmed,
middle-brow vacuity," the two extremes towards which
it presently appears to be heading.[9]

Of Wilson's first two television scripts, one is an
adaptation of a *novella*, "After the Show," from *A Bit
Off the Map*. The other, "The Stranger," suggests many
of the themes and situations of earlier stories, such as
"Heart of Elm" and "A Story of Historical Interest."
The main character in "The Stranger" is Ruby Blacker,
a retired house servant who at seventy-five retains more
zest for life and interest in human beings than most of
the younger people around her. She is devoted to her
lodger, Mr Milroy, the "stranger" whose innocence sets
him apart from the selfish, money-grubbing, social-
climbing people who make up most of Ruby's family.
The plot centres upon the old woman's death from a
stroke, and the legacy she leaves of her life's savings.
This legacy is her relatives' main interest, and she is no
sooner dead than they begin to assess it and try to protect
it from what they naturally suspect is the lodger's similar
interest. Their attitude greatly shocks Mr Milroy, for
(despite much evidence to the contrary) he has preferred
to believe throughout his relationship with the Blackers
that they are really a loving family and that he, because
of his long friendship with Ruby, is like one of the family
too. As for Ruby, she does everything to shield her
"gentleman" from the truth, but as she dies she finds it
necessary to undeceive him. Although her words are
ineffectual—Milroy clings to his innocent faith—her
death and its aftermath do open his eyes. His closing
speech—the last in the play—shows his recognition of
the sordid reality represented by the Blackers. But
mingled with this recognition and cutting across the
bitterness of his tone is the insistent belief that not all

humanity is like them. This, rather melodramatically rendered, is familiar Wilsonian didacticism. But earlier some minor characters, like Albert Merkins, Ruby's grandson through her first marriage, and his wife Violet, who has just had a baby, dramatise the point more effectively, if more subtly. Annie Clayton, a long-suffering old maid tyrannised over by her mother, also shows a little human decency when she offers to help Mr Milroy nurse Ruby after her stroke. Between the good and the positively evil are others who emerge as more foolish than vicious, but a most discordant note is struck when, searching among Mr Milroy's effects, the Blackers discover some pin-up photos of bathing girls. The suddenness of this revelation seems rather gratuit-ously introduced to show that Milroy, for all his goodness, is not so pure after all: like everyone else, he has his vices. But surely his blindness is vice enough in him, and the introduction of the pin-ups jars badly as an unexpected and unwelcome turn of events, rather clumsily used as a springboard for Mr Milroy's final speech.

In many ways, "After the Show" is a better play than "The Stranger," partly because of its lesser dependence upon melodramatic effect and because, like the original story, it involves greater subtleties and refinements of feeling that are competently rendered through dialogue and action. In adapting the story for television, Wilson expands certain scenes and adds others. More characters appear, including Victor, Maurice's uncle, and a new member of his drinking club—stout, fiftyish Jennie, who makes a play for Maurice in the greatly enlarged scene before the end. Both of these characters contribute a good deal to the comedy of the young man's confusion. Among more significant additions is a greater exploita-tion of the "lost youth" theme: against Sylvia's account of her past, the counterpointing of Maurice's longings and aspirations becomes more pertinent; and as she grows in character, his infatuation with her develops, too. Near the end, Maurice even blurts out a declaration of love which Sylvia—with greater sensitivity than we should originally expect—dismisses adroitly and not unkindly with a light kiss on the lips. Finally, Wilson here treats the young man's attempts to behave in a grown-up and responsible fashion with greater sympathy, while still preserving the essential ambivalence of the original. As Maurice's predicament deepens, it also gets clearer, for the struggle between his natural desire for Sylvia and his romantic conception of chivalric behaviour, of "real" love, becomes more definite. Thus, on the whole, "After the Show" is an improvement upon what was already a good short story, mainly because Wilson takes full advantage of the opportunities to rework his material. We may hope for other such adaptations in the future, along with the entirely new plays that have already begun to appear. Wilson promises as much since even more than writers like John Bowen he recognises in this medium a serious intellectual and artistic challenge.[10] But despite the appeal of such drama to literally millions of people otherwise cut off from the theatre and even from books, and despite the discipline that television enforces upon an author's creative imagination, we may yet lament the transitory nature of this art. For, unlike the theatre or cinema, a television play may be pre-empted by a dinner engagement or bridge party which can rob us—forever, perhaps—of the fullest measure of its enjoyment.

Fortunately, radio drama is not liable to losses quite so severe, although its greater limitations as a form must also be cast into the balance. Depending almost entirely upon the spoken word, it is closer to the novel or short story; hence we are scarcely surprised to discover how suitably Wilson develops its techniques. In other ways, too, "Skeletons and Assegais" can be distinguished from the material we have been considering since it is much more directly autobiographical. Its theme, the breaking-up of conventions after the First World War, is very quickly announced by Wilson who, as the subject of a typical radio interview, acts in his own person as both narrator and commentator. The play then proceeds with a number of serio-comic melodramas in which Wilson also participates, only more often now as a schoolboy, living in an hotel with his "grandparents" during his holidays, or visiting with his "uncles and aunts" in the country. With swift facility and customary wit and humour, he presents various situations recalling "Necessity's Child," "Rex Imperator," and other short stories. To evoke the appropriate atmosphere for his settings, he frequently uses gramophone recordings of old songs. But this musical accompaniment does more: like the books that people read in his stories, or like the plays that Maurice and his grandmother attend in "After the Show," they provide a commentary upon the action and the people involved in it. Often they seem to be assegais thrown, as it were, by Wilson himself. For example, the few bars of "How Am I to Know" not only set the scene in 1929 for the domestic row that follows between Wilson's "grandparents," but they also characterise Mrs Wilson's perennial worry about her husband's infidelities. Similarly, "Dance Little Lady" is used satirically to comment upon Marcia, Wilson's aunt, who hates the boredom of family squabbles and only "comes alive" among the smart Oxford undergraduates she meets at certain *gourmets*' restaurants.

Like *Anglo-Saxon Attitudes*, "Skeletons and Assegais" is a story about memory and covers a comparable period of time, beginning in the present and going back as far as 1896. The basic technique of first presenting the effects of a situation and then tracing down their genesis is the same, but Wilson abandons the serial unfolding of events in reversed chronological order that appears so artificial in his novel. Furthermore, from the twin advantages of his own middle age and maturer perspective, he feels freer here to present his family not only less heavily disguised, but also less virulently satirised.

One other aspect of "Skeletons and Assegais" deserves comment. Along with the little dramas that Wilson unfolds as narrator is another drama, integrally related to them. This is the one that develops between Wilson and the person who plays the part of his interviewer, Miss Beatrix Lehmann, or "The Lady Intensely Interested in People." We at once recognise the type (most fully developed in Meg Eliot), and Wilson uses her here for something more than incidental humour or satire. Through her, he tries to anticipate the reactions of his audience, and so correct them, particularly when they over-emphasise the serious aspects of situations which should be taken as only half-serious. As always, Wilson is hostile to sentimental simplifications being imposed upon human experiences. His chief weapon is irony, and as the play progresses we become increasingly aware that his assegais may be thrown in more than one direction.

REFERENCES

1. *Theatre World Annual* (London), VII, June 1955–May 1956, p. 122.
2. *W.W.*, pp. 265 f.
3. See *Through the Looking Glass*, Ch. IV.
4. *M.B.*, p. 111.
5. *M.B.*, p. 110.
6. *Contemporary Theatre*, 1953–1956, New York 1956, p. 84.
7. *W.W.*, p. 265.
8. "The Literary View," 1959, p. 19.
9. "Intellectual on the Aisle," 1959, p. 69.
10. See "The Theatre of Three or Four," 1962, p. 327.

CHAPTER VIII

THE OLD MEN AT THE ZOO

Wilson's fourth novel, *The Old Men at the Zoo*, surprised and disappointed most of his critics: after *The Middle Age of Mrs Eliot*, political satire was hardly anticipated, let alone a novel set in the future. Though politics is occasionally a *leit-motif* in the short stories, reviewers were confused, and their confusion doubtless led many of them to examine the novelty of the satire at its most superficial level. A study of the underlying themes, however, reveals a basic connexion to the earlier novels and much reduces the relative significance of the book's purely political concern.

For, once again, Wilson is preoccupied here with questions of personal versus public responsibility, and especially with the fundamental *response* that is at the heart of both. Such a response, he recognises, accepts the Self as wholly real and the Other as existing in the same way; that is, not as a mere object, but as a reality equal in being to the Self. Or, to use Buber's terms, a response occurs when an *I* and a *Thou* enter into dialogue, a dialogue from which it is impossible to emerge unchanged. In assuming any public responsibility, therefore, a person must be capable of making and eliciting a response, of entering into dialogue. Without this capacity, his "responsibility" becomes an abstraction, an empty imperative, that dehumanises him in the same proportion as it reduces his awareness of the world.

In *The Old Men at the Zoo*, Wilson explores this theme on a scale he has not previously attempted and with a technique he has not fully perfected. He adopts the form of the novel set slightly in the future, like Nevil Chute's *On the Beach*, and imagines the history of the London Zoo for the years 1970–73, during which occur at least one conventional war and one (undescribed) liberation. Since his real interest is not in external trappings, but in perennial human problems, the novel might as well be set in the present—unless (as it happens) there is some other reason for this fantasy of the future. By taking the London Zoo and its four successive administrations as his central focus, Wilson contrasts the instinctual and rational motivations of human behaviour and suggests—though without perfect clarity—how a proper human response should involve both. The Directors of the Zoo are so governed by some pet project—a product of their particular monomanias—that they eventually become incapable of responding adequately, or at all, to the other demands made upon them as director, husband, father, or friend. The political, military, and economic crises that confront them—extreme developments of the anxieties Britain has been experiencing ever since the Second World War—function mainly, then, to intensify these concerns.

Serving under each one of the Directors, and thus furnishing an essential continuity of events, is the narrator, Simon Carter, who is the Zoo's young Administrative Secretary. In character and disposition he most closely resembles Peter Lord or Robin Middleton from Wilson's earlier works. While the Directors at the outset of their regimes appear pretty far gone in their monomania, Carter's deterioration is gradual. An actually and potentially responsive human being at the start, he identifies himself ever more closely with an ideal of administrative responsibility founded upon principles of "exactitude" and order. He thus steadily allows himself to lose touch with the two major sources that feed his instinctual life and provide his greatest pleasures—his work as an amateur naturalist, and his enjoyment of family life with his wife and children. By the end of the novel, after the fourth and most sinister regime has ended, Carter's once promising responsiveness and acute perception are so completely lost that, ironically, he qualifies for a Directorship himself and, indeed, begins actively campaigning for the job.

In many ways the opening episode of the book becomes a central focus for subsequent events. Derek Filson, a young keeper, is killed by a sick giraffe; and though it is never definitely established as fact, rumour has it that during the attack Filson's testicles were crushed by the giraffe's hoofs. But surpassing the horror of the accident itself is the response to it from almost every quarter. Dr Leacock, the Zoo's Director, views the incident as a possible asset in propagating his scheme for a National Reserve outside London to replace Regent's Park, but for the moment he wishes to avoid any unfavourable publicity that might jeopardise his forthcoming television show about this project. Sir Robert Falcon, Curator of Mammals and once Britain's most famous explorer, is willing to become a scapegoat for the affair—a signal gesture of his despair and of his disregard for the present order of things—but he refuses to carry through his official responsibility. He will neither reprimand his chief keeper, a colourful Zoo character named Strawson, nor see to it that appropriate precautions are taken in the future. Even the boy's parents fail to respond with proper concern for what has happened. Mr Filson, representing a family tradition of keepers going back to the Zoo's foundation, is anxious to avoid scandal and, with his wife, wishes for still other reasons simply to let matters rest.

In the midst of all this expediency and evasion, Carter, though in no way involved with the accident, tries to launch an investigation. He believes he is moved by a sincere regard for human life, based more upon the concrete reality of young Filson's suffering than upon his own slight acquaintance with the boy. He does not recognise, however, that his concern is partly an abstraction of his self-righteous conscience, or priggishness (it is this "puritan conscience" that dogs him throughout the book and finally undoes him). Also motivating him is a desire to revenge the muddle that caused the accident and thus violated his ideal of administrative competence. In short, the rational origins of Carter's behaviour tend to overbalance the instinctive and compassionate ones, "sterilising" the event for him, as Buber would say, so that eventually he cannot feel its *personal* address any longer. When, in fact, he confronts the elder Filsons with plans that run counter to their wishes, his quest for moral justice wavers before their more solidly based longing not to be hurt further, and he drops the investigation.

Carter's dwindling capacity for human relationships and his final revulsion from them altogether are reflected in his experiences with all the Directors under whom he works, but primarily with Dr Leacock. Under Leacock's plans for a National Reserve, where the animals may enjoy the fine compromise of "Limited Liberty," Carter will serve jointly as Warden of native British wildlife and as Administrative Secretary for the whole park. In this way, he hopes to reconcile pleasure with duty and so end the "bifurcation" of his life.[1] Opposing Leacock's scheme, however, are several trustees and Falcon, who cherishes the Zoo's Victorian charm and wants to salvage at least this much of the old order of things. When rich, old Lord Godmanchester, President of the Zoological Society, at last offers to finance the Reserve himself, all obstacles suddenly vanish for Leacock. He jumps at the offer, though he is fully aware that Godmanchester wants to use the Reserve to serve his own political ambitions. He throws off Carter's moral uneasiness with great irritability, and fails to see how vulnerable he

becomes in other respects. As a result, once his scheme
has helped put Godmanchester into office, and then
threatens to turn into a political liability, the Reserve
and Leacock are doomed.

Further undermining the Director's position is the way
fanatical devotion to his brainchild usurps the deeper
obligations to his human family, especially to his
daughter Harriet, whose nymphomaniac tendencies are
an indirect consequence of his own emotional and sexual
immaturity. As work on the Reserve begins, and Leacock and his wife move up from London to take charge,
Harriet is legally restricted to their supervision because
of the latest in her series of misdemeanours: like the
animals, she also is to enjoy only "Limited Liberty." It
is during this period that Carter, who has surrendered
his scruples and allowed himself to be brought into the
project, first encounters Harriet's demands upon him,
demands that he is unable to satisfy. Nor is it her sexual
demands alone that he is unable to meet: he cannot—
nor can anyone else, it appears—make the kind of
response that would provide a human focus for her and
so temper the animalism to which she is being driven in
her search for satisfying relationships. Hence, the compassion she feels for an escaped lynx which her father
orders to be shot (to avert, he believes, any public outcry
against his Reserve) foreshadows her own death. Unable
to thrive under her present confinement, and without the
prospect of some rewarding human intercourse, she turns
in despair to her pet mastiff, which kills her.

The manner of Harriet's death gives Godmanchester
all he needs to relax her father's stubborn hold on the
Reserve. In this situation Carter can force the weapon
out of Godmanchester's hands by boldly proclaiming
what really happened, but Leacock makes him consider
the possible effect of the truth upon his wife, who believes
her daughter has been killed by another escaped animal.
Such confrontation, based upon meeting Mrs Leacock

in a way that her husband refuses to do—as a person, as someone equally capable of adult behaviour—proves too much for Carter, as had the earlier encounter with Mrs Filson, and he again backs away from that responsibility. The physical violence of Harriet's death is thus paralleled on many levels by the violence done to the possibilities of human dialogue and (in her father's humiliation) to human dignity.

These episodes, which cover about half the book, suggest Carter's further deterioration and through him, the deterioration of his world. The breakdown of responsibility in the sphere of individual human relations corresponds to a similar breakdown in the administrative responsibility for the Zoo—which near the end almost turns into a Roman circus—and ultimately to the failure of civilised nations to rise above a politics of power upheld by the use of nuclear weapons. This last development of Wilson's theme, however sensational it appears, is really the least basic, but it seems to have sidetracked a good many critics, especially in America. Assuming that *The Old Men at the Zoo* is modelled upon Orwell's *1984* or Huxley's *Brave New World*, they failed to examine the novel adequately in the context of Wilson's other work. Hence, they mistook the political theme for the major one and complained, like Phoebe Adams in *The Atlantic Monthly*, that there was no "clear prophetic pattern."[2] Comparisons to Orwell and Huxley, though not odious, are a little misleading. Wilson's greatest debt is to an older author, someone whose wit is more like his own, and whose satire is more subtle and more complex than either Orwell's or Huxley's. There seems little doubt that the chief model for this novel is *Gulliver's Travels*.

Wilson's satire, like Swift's, is political at only one level, and not the most profound one at that. Likewise, Wilson traces the development of his narrator from a person able to respond with benevolence and compassion, to someone thoroughly the victim of his own

G

pride, and he shows this development as a progression through four "voyages" into fantasy. Perhaps the most striking similarity between Carter and Gulliver, in this respect, is the relative ease with which they accommodate themselves to their changing surroundings. When Leacock's Reserve ends in fiasco and his rival, Falcon, is appointed Director, Carter at first thinks of resigning from the Zoo in a gesture of protest. But vanity and ambition, masked as duty, dissuade him, and he remains at his post. Though Falcon's reactionary policy runs counter to everything that his Administrative Secretary believes in, Carter works on and eventually participates with pleasure in what he had previously opposed and even despised. Gulliver, gradually acclimatised to the scale of Lilliput, rather quickly adjusts to a directly opposite scale on his next voyage, falling into Brobdingnagian evaluations of size, distance, and still more important kinds of perspective. This facility reaches its culmination during Gulliver's last voyage when he tries to imitate the Houyhnhnms—rejecting his own human nature as distorted by the Yahoos, and failing to see in the horses an opposite but equally serious distortion. So Carter, in the administration of Wilson's Zoo, adapts himself to one directorship after another until, like Gulliver, he loses all sense of the necessary balance in human nature. Under the Zoo's fourth and most notorious Director, the kindly collaborator Dr Englander, he begins to yearn for a life based solely upon rational controls (epitomised by Englander's policy of "competence, good sense, and above all, moderation"),[3] and to covet the power that such rationalism affords.

Other comparisons with Swift's satire, such as the Laputians' absorption in science and Dr Charles Langley-Beard's devotion to vertebrate anatomy, may with so little difficulty be multiplied that it is curious how critics have been misled in the way already indicated.[4] True,

Wilson's apparent concern with Britain's actual political future does lend itself to some confusion. To judge from recent events, Britain is more disturbed by being excluded from the European Economic Community than by any pressure to enter it. And no country, she or any other, is likely in 1970 to arm herself exclusively with nuclear weapons, as Wilson prophesies! But we are hardly asked to take this crystal gazing seriously:[5] far more important in the novel is the theme of human responsibility.

What is different is the technique. *The Old Men at the Zoo* inverts the pattern of Wilson's previous novels and gives full bent to his satiric impulse. Like the other heroes, Simon Carter has at first a remarkable gift of irony, including self-irony, which makes him an excellent agent for satire. But in the unfolding of events he steadily changes, like Gulliver, from the instrument of satire to its object. Instead of becoming aware, like Bernard Sands or Meg Eliot, of his delusions and self-deceptions, he falls more and more their victim, rejecting whatever help is offered him by his wife and by others. It is perhaps just here that the novel in launching its most vigorous attack suggests also its weakest aspect. For, as in *Anglo-Saxon Attitudes*, Wilson again crowds his canvas with an overabundance of incident and detail, but despite its wealth of characters *The Old Men at the Zoo* suffers from the absence of a norm usually found in satire. If, for Wilson, the norm for human behaviour derives from a balance between the instinctual and rational sources of our actions, then his presentation of this norm, presumably in the idea of "Limited Liberty," is travestied in the characterisations of Leacock and Carter, who are also its chief proponents! Irony used in this way becomes self-defeating. Several minor characters, such as young Filson's fiancée, reveal fragments of Wilson's belief in a limited kind of personal heroism: but they are otherwise too severely crippled by satire to impress us very much. This may be why some readers think that

Wilson believes all people are "extraordinarily nasty"[6] (the same thing used to be said of Swift). But then such readers entirely overlook evidence to the contrary from his other novels and the bits of evidence—admittedly meagre—from the present one. Wilson is no misanthrope, and it is an inadequate reading of satire which takes an author's criticism of our human feelings as a sign of complete disgust. More to the point is the corrective vision that satire tries to provide. Despite his frequent disclaimers that he has no "philosophy of life", Wilson more and more reveals a concern for the future of human beings becoming able to respond to one another freely, with neither dogma, nor guilt, nor an unbitted lust for power obstructing or perverting the way. There is no telling, of course, what form his next novel will take, though if he retains the satire of *The Old Men* we may hope that he fully perfects his technique and clarifies his vision.

REFERENCES

1. *O.M.Z.*, pp. 156–7.
2. "Books in Review," *The Atlantic Monthly*, ccviii, Nov. 1961, p. 191.
3. *O.M.Z.*, p. 321.
4. John Wain in the *Observer*, 24 Sep. 1961, p. 30, is a notable exception; and in America, Paul Pickrel in *Harper's Magazine*, Nov. 1961, pp. 110–11.
5. Cp. Wilson's headnote: "the events described . . . are utterly improbable," *O.M.Z.*, p. 6.
6. *Time Magazine*, 3 Nov. 1961, p. 86.

CHAPTER IX

CRITICISM

We may derive a writer's theory of literature in three ways: inductively from his own work, deductively from what he says about the work of others, and—most directly—from the forthright exposition of his views in lectures or books on the subject. Wilson's theory is available in all three ways. Ever since his early success as a short-story writer, and later on as a novelist and play-wright, he has increasingly contributed articles and reviews to leading journals and newspapers in Great Britain and abroad. In the fall of 1960, because of his distinction as both writer and critic, he was invited to give the Ewing Lectures at the University of California at Los Angeles, where he chose for his topic, "On Being a Novelist." From such sources as these, together with his stories and novels, we can therefore construct a co-herent theory of fiction that bears significantly on Wilson's own work and that is important to the total body of contemporary literary criticism as well.

Wilson divides his Ewing Lectures into three related subjects: the Source of the Novel, the Process, and the Purpose. Since he has frequently asserted that he has found the ideas of Freud extremely influential, we are prepared for his view that the origins of the novel have much to do with the writer's unconscious. His whole approach, in fact, reveals this psychoanalytical bias; for example, the novelist (he says) must "destroy" himself, he must dissolve his personality "in a series of memories and echoes and imaginations and visions," in order to get at the true sources of his work. Wilson's own starting point is that the novelist's vision is essentially connected with other human beings. An historically accurate observation,[1] the idea is developed here apropos of the novelist's "childhood" vision of life, his partially unresolved mental conflicts, and his moral or metaphysical preoccupations.

The childhood vision, as Wilson defines it, is doubtless his most interesting and, in these lectures, perhaps his most original contribution to literary theory. A novelist's imagination, he says, is directly and inherently related to a child's. The childhood vision is, of course, insufficient in itself, and Wilson later explains how a mature view is needed to supplement, or rather to organise, the child's way of looking at the world. The absence of any childhood vision, on the other hand, is bad, and he notes in some of the novels of Galsworthy, C. P. Snow, and James G. Cozzens "a quality of plum-puddingness or suet-puddingness that belongs to overpurposeful maturity." One must not be a Peter Pan, he cautions, but "this constant reaching out for maturity in itself has its dangers."

Childhood visions are of two sorts. The first is the kind of fantasy a child has when he takes isolated bits of experience and, by shaping them into patterns, makes games of life. This process Wilson calls *fusion*, and he demonstrates it from a passage in "Raspberry Jam," where Johnnie endows his toys with the voices and other characteristics of people whom he has met or read about.[2] Rodney Brent's monologue at the end of "Necessity's Child" demonstrates the other kind of vision that Wilson calls self-dramatisation.[3] It is a later form of childhood fantasy which occurs at about the age of thirteen, supplanting the earlier one after two or three years and itself, in Wilson's opinion, an important stage in the history of the imagination. It is basically the power to assimilate or to identify oneself with many different people. In the first instance, Wilson says, "you are standing away, you are putting people together, putting phrases together that you hear; you are making up dialogue, you are making up character. But in the other you are putting yourself inside, you are dramatizing each person that you come upon." Both kinds are important to the novelist because, apart from supplying the important bits of objective, concrete reality that the novel demands, they serve to restore the function of imagination among many who have lost it in the process of growing up. In so far as the novel is not an "intellectual thesis"—and in Wilson's view it is not, though it may and should say intellectually serious things—it depends for its success upon touching the reader's emotions and sensibilities; that is, by awakening the reader's imagination, the novelist stimulates his intellect as no other art (except possibly the drama) can do. There is the danger, of course, always to be avoided, Wilson says, of retaining this childhood vision too long into adult life, when it may become a kind of self-protective wall, a form of adult whimsy, such as he satirises in the story "Crazy Crowd." All the novels of Nancy Mitford have this "coterie" feeling about them. In their different ways, Virginia Woolf's *The Waves* and E. M. Forster's *The Longest Journey* seem also to suffer from a refusal to "go out to meet the world." The connexions between separate human beings are there, but they are too inbred, too insulated. As a result, these novels have less and less to do with the actual world, which should always be, Wilson suggests, somewhere near the centre of the one that the writer creates.

In fashioning this world, the novelist must use a number of tricks to deceive the reader, to make him accept the reality of his fiction. The writer must first, of course, thoroughly deceive himself so that he believes: "(*a*) that the book is worth writing; (*b*) that it is credible; and finally, (*c*) that it is not only credible but the only reality that there is." This fictitious deception and self-

deception is something that the novelist shares with other
sorts of people, usually those regarded as rather dis-
reputable types: the gossip, the confidence-trickster, the
professional diner-out, and the professional failed person.
All of them must assume an innate scepticism in people
and learn to overcome it by anticipating criticisms,
attending carefully to objective details, and studiously
applying the rules of one-upmanship.

The discussion of the various modes of deception, or
fiction, particularly as used by the professional failed
person, leads Wilson to consider the neurotic conflict
which he believes underlies the novelist's work but
which is not always easy for him to recognise. It derives
from some imperfectly resolved crisis in his life that tries
to work itself out symbolically. This is not a psychologically curative process, but it does provide an important part of a writer's motive energy. As an example,
Wilson discusses Dickens's bitter experience at the
blacking factory. Had Dickens not had the courage to
write about this difficult period in *David Copperfield*, his
deep resentment against life, against the aristocracy—
his fear of not being taken for a gentleman—might have
led him to create only such heroes as he himself wished
to be. But unlike the "walking gentlemen and genteel
figures" of his early novels, the heroes of his later work
acquired the flesh and blood qualities of great fiction.
They became dandies, like Eugene Wrayburn, who
could well express the author's hostility towards society.
But Dickens could not have made his hero the sort of
aristocrat that he hated most when he began to write
if he had not got over the profound resentment of having
himself been made to work—as no gentlemen, he felt,
ought to be made to work—at the blacking factory.
Now Dickens was conscious of this trauma, but Wilson
suspects that there was a deeper conflict, one of which
he was not conscious, which found an outlet in his
fiction, especially later on. He refused to face, or could

not face, the fact that he was a man who needed domestic life—a family around him—but that he was at the same time a very sensual person. This, Wilson believes, explains why he gradually allowed his heroes to have some of the sensuality that he would not confront as part of his own nature.[4]

Speaking of his personal experience, Wilson recognises that in *Hemlock and After* and again in *The Middle Age of Mrs Eliot* he is trying to resolve a conflict between his own liberal and humane attitude towards life and certain deep-seated, cruel instincts. This conflict, we recall, is what finally kills Bernard Sands and what threatens to destroy Meg Eliot, when she discovers her driving need to dominate the people around her. But since he is conscious of this conflict, Wilson doubts whether it is really the deepest one within him. This, he thinks, may be related rather to the shock of his mother's sudden death when he was fifteen. His father's death some years later hardly affected him as much. Nor did the experience of returning home from London one Saturday afternoon to discover his landlady, whom he much enjoyed living with, lying on the floor in a para-lytic seizure. "I have written about the death of that old woman in three different forms in my writing," he says. "I have also written about somebody dying in a hotel, but I've made it my father and never my mother." He confesses that he does not fully understand all this him-self, but thinks that the conflict between his humane attitude and cruel instinct is, like Dickens's blacking factory, much too general, and that there is something far deeper working itself out in his fiction. The suggestion is worth pursuing because it is very important to his novels, where women invariably demonstrate much greater heroism than the men who are the heroes. This is true of Ella Sands, Dollie Stokesay, Meg Eliot, and even Martha Carter. Wilson saw great courage in his mother—much more than in his father, whom he nevertheless liked. Moreover, he greatly admired the youngest of his five brothers, to whose wit and tenderness, histrionic prowess and creative fantasy, combined with an extremely effeminate manner, Wilson says he owes the pervasiveness of the feminine in his work. Some struggle between the masculine and feminine natures, as Wilson consciously or unconsciously recognises and values them, thus seems to be going on within him. The homosexuals who are major characters in two novels, and who appear conspicuously in all four, manifest this conflict most clearly: but it is significant that the nature of homosexuality itself—apart from various social problems that are connected with it—has not yet received direct and intensive treatment. Instead, the conflict seems to be working itself out more subtly and perhaps less consciously in these comparisons of feminine and masculine strengths. In any event, according to this Freudian view, such conflict surely gives shape—"symbolic shape"—to the work of all serious writers. In his study of Émile Zola, as in his shorter studies of Dickens and Samuel Butler, Wilson therefore pays considerable attention to the particular forms of trauma that these novelists experienced in childhood and adolescence, and especially to the ways that these experiences work themselves out in their fiction.

From childhood vision, then, the novelist gets dialogue, description, atmosphere; from inner conflict he gets drama and suspense. But something further is necessary to all this—a moral or metaphysical preoccupation that contributes intellectual substance and an adult view of the world. Wilson's moral preoccupation has been with the collapse of liberalism in our time, a view that derives from his emotionally less intense but intellectually far more stimulating contacts with people after his mother's death who became for him a kind of substitute family. By contrast, the short story, he believes, can make do with solely the other requisites for fiction: an ear for dialogue, an eye for description, and a sense of drama, or conflict. But however this tends to belittle the story form—and in actual practice, as we have seen, Wilson's stories often reveal a definite, mature point of view—still the novel contains much more "that must be meditated, that must be thought about, intellectually thought about, hard." Characteristically betraying a histrionic bias, Wilson does not dwell on this point but at once stipulates that no matter how serious his intellectual preoccupation may be, the writer must quickly "go back and recharge all that with life and with drama" if his novel is to be any good. Further discussion of this position he reserves for his third lecture on the Purpose of the Novel.

The second lecture, on the Process of writing novels, describes how a novelist actually puts his novel together. Wilson personally lays much emphasis upon note-taking, the means through which he convinces himself that the materials of his fiction—the characters, the plot and sub-plots, the topography, time-sequence, and so forth— are indeed credible. From his detailed discussion of these materials one or two major considerations emerge concerning the function of objective detail and the techniques of narration. Once the novelist has settled upon the main themes of his novel and the appropriate vehicles for them in his characters and their distinctive voices, he must then build up around them a real world of objects. The need for concrete objects, Wilson believes, corresponds to the "degree of romanticism," or "intense passion," that writers such as Balzac and Zola felt in contrast, say, to Henry James, who experienced less violent internal conflict about life than they. He argues further that all psychological novels from James's time onwards which depend heavily upon the interior monologue have as one of their weaknesses "the gradual dispersion, the melting away, of concrete objects which ought to surround the character." From what he demonstrates in his own work, as well as from what he says here, it is clear that Wilson is closer to the French writers he mentions than to James, both in artistic temperament, it would seem, and in his vivid use of every sort of concrete detail—of actual time and place and all the paraphernalia of contemporary English life.

This sensibility may be what has caused Wilson to brood at some length upon the techniques of narration and to conclude, despite the competence displayed in his own work, that he has not yet discovered any entirely successful one. The various forms of omniscient author, first-person narrator, interior monologue, all appear to have the disadvantages of either the unwarranted obtrusion of the author into the action or, conversely, his too great detachment from it. Wilson is quite right to uphold this aspect of the novel, in contrast to the denigrations evinced by such writers as E. M. Forster, whom he cites. Many a novel has been marred—often needlessly—by its narration, as for example *The Middle Age of Mrs Eliot*, where Wilson, anticipating our own comments, relates his difficulty in deciding to switch narrators two-thirds of the way through the book. He gives his reasons for the decision, but concludes that it was undoubtedly a mistake, despite his feeling that Meg's voice might be tiring to the reader by then or that she should at last be seen through someone else's eyes. He mentions other examples, too, from the novels of Lawrence Durrell and C. P. Snow to demonstrate the difficulties of first- and third-person narration; however, he seems to miss the essential point that, having decided upon the most suitable form of narration, the novelist's job is no longer to ponder techniques but to sustain his craft. Wilson may regard the interior monologue as "the most heavy, ugly, and cumbrous form that has yet been invented"—a "disaster," in short—but the fact is that he has achieved his greatest artistic success by using it. If *Mrs Eliot* falls short of complete success, it is mainly because of an error in tactics. His objection to the form, moreover, reveals a familiar prejudice: by using the interior monologue, the writer may get "further and further away from the dramatics" and then have a hard time getting back to them. But surely this must be a problem of the novelist's skill, not of the technique itself.

Discussing the Purpose of Novels in the last of the Ewing Lectures, Wilson considers anew that the urge to write is a phenomenon common among many different kinds of people. Many are called—but there are siren voices, too. And of course there are other professions, such as acting, also well suited to the talents of the "born novelist." But given a predisposition to histrionics, for which the novel, among many other things, may serve as an outlet, what else is there that distinguishes the Purpose? Not money, certainly: he attacks the materialist arguments of some novelists as ignoble and probably insincere. Nor is "doing good" an acceptable motive. Wilson is not a partisan of the Leavis school of moral criticism or like D. H. Lawrence an advocate of the prophetic voice of literature. Despite the moral or metaphysical preoccupation which he says a serious novelist must have, he feels that any dogmatic or prophetic approach by the writer will ultimately prove destructive to his art. "However one may build up a strong tradition for critical purposes [as Leavis does in *The Great Tradition*, which in this sense is 'most valuable'], writers are not here as sort of soul doctors to the community."

What, then, are writers here for? Wilson takes up his position next to that of Jane Austen, and cites her defence of the novel as "only some work in which the greatest powers of the mind are displayed, in which the most thorough knowledge of human nature, the happiest delineation of its varieties, the liveliest effusions of wit and humour, are conveyed to the world in the best chosen language."[5] To do all this—to present life imaginatively experienced and aptly expressed—is the novelist's task. The Source and the Purpose of writing novels are thus closely connected. But Wilson adds here some further remarks about the rendering of an "individualistic pattern of life." Using Proust as his example, he says that the only thing that one can feel while writing a book is that "life is there simply to provide these juxtapositions [of events] and these moments in time together to create a work of art." Through art we find meaning in life and so conquer time, life's destroyer. Wilson hastens to add that, taken by itself, this philosophy is insufficient: but for the artist *in the act of creating*, it is the only possible answer to the question about the purpose of his art.

The individuality of the writer's vision is therefore basic. This is true both historically, since the novel is an expression of middle-class individualism and freedom (as opposed to aristocratic tradition); and intrinsically, since it is an unfettered mode of organising experience (as opposed to the drama, which begins and ends in ritual). Should the novel die, as indeed it may, Wilson believes that its death will come about by some kind of "hardening of the arteries." That is, in a society like that of contemporary Britain, which seems headed towards a fixed hierarchical structure based upon a tyrannical system of education, the novel quite possibly will be stifled as a form of free expression. In his opinion, this is already happening in the Soviet Union, where the form lacks any real flexibility or individuality, and where the connexion between other human beings and the author—the very heart of the novel—appears to be missing. But it is precisely in this stress upon individual vision and the connexion with other human beings that we may discover Wilson's notion of the novel's true moral function. It is a very important one. Through the novelist's peculiar feeling or reverence for the uniqueness of everyone he meets—regardless of whether they arouse his

love or hate, admiration or ridicule—we may preserve
something of our own respect for the "absolute independence of people's special qualities." And as long as
we respect a person's individuality, then just so long,
perhaps, will we hang on to those forms of society which
serve human beings, and resist those other forms in
which human beings are used to serve society.

The theory of fiction presented here underlies Wilson's
practice both as a novelist and a critic, and is consistent
with all his literary criticism from the introductory study
of Émile Zola, written in 1951, to his most recent review
in the *Observer*. Thus the opening paragraph of his book
on Zola argues the importance for the literary artist of
his emotional stresses in childhood and adolescence,
especially as these stresses may derive from an increasing
awareness of "the dreadful gulf that lies between his
fantasy world . . . and the vast, uncomforting desert of
the society in which he must live."[6] This theoretical
position is reiterated and later expanded to account for
the development of the writer after his early maturity.
In Chapter IV, for example, Wilson examines the profound change in Zola's work as the result of his liaison
in middle age with Jeanne Rozerat. This psychological
approach has at bottom an aspect that explains both its
great strength and its great weakness as literary criticism.
Its weakness is that it involves the critic in a great deal
of speculation about cause and effect, leading him
frequently to embark upon exciting but necessarily
tentative explorations of the subject's unconscious. Given
the equivocal nature of the evidence they depend upon,
such critics inevitably fall short of complete assent from
the reader. The suppositions that colour Wilson's interpretation of the early liaison with Alexandrine Meley,
and Mme Zola's acceptance of it,[7] are only a few
examples of the sort of thing which undermines an otherwise lively and provocative thesis put forward about the
writer's early life and its influence upon his novels.

In so far as this psychological approach stimulates a fuller response from the critic, however, it may be useful to both Freudians and non-Freudians alike. The critic's responsibility is a public one in precisely the same sense defined at the beginning of the last chapter; his approach to his subject, therefore, should be in the form of entering into dialogue with it so that an appropriate, fruitful *relation* may begin. His response—*engagement* is perhaps a better term in this context—will necessarily involve greater sympathy and more direct critical concern than the ideal of complete detachment aimed at by some modern writers, but it need not imply any lack of perspective. This personalist view of criticism is not to be confused with the vague, subjective impressionism that late nineteenth- and early twentieth-century men of letters delighted in and that Wilson, citing Gosse, specifically objects to in his Ewing Lectures. The critic's greater personal response does not presuppose losing sight of his subject: on the contrary, he must pay extremely close attention to its unique reality if the dialogue he desires is to occur. Otherwise, he is likely to fall into either the monologue of belles-lettristic critics who ignore the reality, or the dogmatising of those whose tendency is to violate it.

From a personal engagement in his subject the critic produces an unusually lively commentary that has among its virtues a sense of immediacy, of relevance, that is essential to any vital criticism. Its most obvious expression may be the histrionics that Wilson practises now and again in his study of Zola; for instance, when he imagines how the Rougon-Macquart novels must have affected their readers. But the critic's engagement can find less extravagant, more profoundly moving expressions than this. In Wilson's criticism they appear not only in his volume on Zola, but frequently in the many articles and reviews for *Encounter*, the *Spectator*, the *Observer*, and other leading periodicals that he has contributed to ever since his early recognition as a writer with something worth saying.

It is in his criticism of Dickens, whom he most esteems and loves, as well as in his comments upon living contemporaries, that we get Wilson's most personal utterance—and with it the most exacting test of this personalist theory. Occasionally, as in his review of John Wain's *Sprightly Running*,[8] his intense sympathy with the subject—indeed, his very considerable identification with it—may tend unduly to colour his perspective: but with characteristic self-awareness and honesty he at once raises this very question. Having alerted both the reader and himself, he then tries to ascertain what in his view is valuable about Wain's book, and why. Of course, such personal revelation as he makes in the process might be thought presumptuous in a writer of less reputation. Wilson's stance is clearly that of a well-known novelist comparing autobiographical notes with a brother novelist of equal stature, though of much different background and output, and discovering a shared experience of great significance for them both. But from his earliest criticism onwards Wilson has never hesitated to confront his subject personally. In his "London Letter" written for the *American Mercury Magazine* (1951), we not only read a comment upon the England of that time; we hear also the voice of a new, perceptive writer talking about himself and his *milieu* and not—as so often happens—being carried away by either subject. Again, in a review of Christopher Hassall's biography of Sir Edward Marsh,[9] Wilson devotes over half of his article to a detailed account of his few personal encounters with Marsh before his death. This surely would seem presumptuous, even for someone who was so well known as Wilson was by then; except that it is all part of the basic criticism of the book. For despite his long and close acquaintance with Sir Edward, Hassall fails to convey his friend as he really was, an actual person; and this Wilson, from his

H

own admittedly circumscribed experience, tries to provide.

Although, as we have said, personal engagement with a subject runs the risk of fostering certain uncritical predispositions, still the very depth of this engagement and the strength of his convictions may enable the critic, paradoxically, to evaluate the weaknesses and failures of his subject more justly than others who seek merely to disparage or to denigrate. The condition, of course, is that the critic must remain constantly aware of his own predilections—the position Wilson takes, for example, in his essay on "The Heroes and Heroines of Dickens." In "Charles Dickens: A Haunting," he is still more obviously and completely personal. Writing while *The Old Men at the Zoo* was exercising a different, obsessive pull upon his imagination, he only half apologises for an essay that he calls "unashamedly subjective." The reason for less than a full apology— assuming that one is really needed—is that "the constant and haunting pressure of Dickens's created world" is strong enough to offset the other dominant preoccupation, certainly for the purposes of what pretends to be no more than an outline of an analysis. Actually, Wilson here wants to track down some of the causes of this constant pressure, or at least to follow up some clues, and for such an undertaking his peculiar situation would seem as propitious as any other, and perhaps better. At any rate, in the process he gives us both a personally revealing but also objectively argued account of where the Dickens "magic" may lie. He swiftly dismisses current academic opinion concerning the artistic excellence of *David Copperfield*, *Great Expectations*, and *Hard Times*, and instead puts forward the thesis that Dickens's power may best be understood not by any "conventional canons of greatness" but rather through other, more deeply-searching criteria. He acknowledges the usefulness of Freudian and Marxist theories, but (significantly) notes their limitations. An approach through Dickens's "miraculous" eye and ear is likewise too restricted. His preference is for the examination of the "symbolic unities" of individual novels, in the manner of Edmund Wilson or Lionel Trilling. "I have no doubt at all," he says, "that if we must assess Dickens's greatness on the basis of any artistic unity, it is to this deeper level rather than to the more conventional technical or moral surfaces that we must go."[10] From this he concludes that "in its working out of symbol and in its unity of atmosphere" *Little Dorrit* is the most perfect of Dickens's novels and hence much worthier than *Hard Times* to be placed alongside *Emma*, *Middlemarch*, and *The Secret Agent* as the greatest English novels of their times.

But the "if" in the sentence just quoted signals more than a rhetorical construction; it begins a very important qualification. For Wilson is unwilling to settle for any of the criteria of artistic unity to explain the greatest power of Dickens's work, its specifically haunting quality. He suggests, rather, that it is the recurrent situations, images, and symbols, found in all of Dickens's books especially from *Bleak House* onwards, which, taken together, work this fascination upon the reader. Among the most compelling of these recurrent situations and symbols are travelling, feasts, and home. In their ambiguous presentation as "pursuit-flight" or "home-prison," they have a particular appeal to the twentieth-century mind, troubled as it is with similar conflicts. This argument goes a long way to redeem from the academic dustbin many of Dickens's weaker novels, bringing our attention to them in the same way that the Shakespearian critic must take account of such "imperfect" or "lesser" plays as *Timon of Athens* and *All's Well That Ends Well*. At the same time, and most far-reaching in its implications, the argument demands that we re-examine the canons of conventional contemporary criticism, and joins with the criticism of others, like

R. P. Blackmur, who has maintained that "wholeness, preconceived, is a prison into which the mind is not compelled to thrust itself."[11] By keeping out of the prison, we may, then, find room for the greater breadth as well as depth of our personal vision.

REFERENCES

1. Cp. "Evil in the English Novel," 1962, pp. 1079 f.
2. *W.S.*, pp. 146 f.
3. *S.D.D.*, p. 120.
4. See also "The Heroes and Heroines of Dickens," 1961, pp. 7–18.
5. *Northanger Abbey*, Ch. V.
6. *E.Z.*, p. 1.
7. See *E.Z.*, p. 20.
8. The *Observer*, 16 Sep. 1962, p. 22.
9. The *Spectator*, 12 Jun. 1959, p. 861.
10. The *Critical Quarterly*, II, 1960, p. 105.
11. *Form and Value in Modern Poetry*, New York, 1957, p. 83.

CHAPTER X

RETROSPECT AND PROSPECT

From "On Being a Novelist," the topic of his Ewing Lectures, Wilson has become increasingly concerned with the history of Good and Evil in English fiction. This was the subject of his Northcliffe Lectures in 1961 and again of his Sir Leslie Stephen Lecture in 1963, where he concentrated upon Samuel Richardson, the writer from whose work he traces several traditions of the English and Continental novel. Here, the subject may serve as one means, among others, of evaluating Wilson's own contributions to literature; of determining what his peculiar gifts are, and how he has developed them; and, finally, of estimating what promise he yet holds as an important figure in contemporary letters.

The major intellectual problem for the novelist, Wilson now believes, is how "to wed his sense of a transcendent evil and good to the fully felt social novel that the English have constructed in their great tradition."[1] He notes the efforts of his contemporaries—Graham Greene, William Golding, Ivy Compton-Burnett, and others—to deal with the problem. Although each one makes his approach from a different position, none of their attempts is wholly satisfactory. Of the three writers named, Golding and Miss Compton-Burnett are closest to Wilson in their shared agnosticism: but however successful Miss Compton-Burnett is in incorporating a sense of evil within the traditional kind of novel, the evil itself, while real enough, does not encompass the full reality that Wilson sees about us to-day. To the extent that Golding does so in *Free Fall*, his novel, though ultimately a failure, is more fruitful. Wilson's own efforts in *Hemlock and After* are complicated, he says, by the twentieth-century novelist's need to use psychological explanations for his characters' actions, and this seriously qualifies the success of such characters as Hubert Rose and Mrs Curry. We may add that a similar argument has been used by others to explain the difficulty of writing contemporary tragedy: robbed of the sense of mystery that lies at the heart of the great classics (Greek or Elizabethan), the writer has had to abandon the form altogether in favour of the problem play, or else seek mysteries as have not yet been explained away by psychoanalysis or related sciences. Perhaps such considerations as these have been responsible for the changing mode of Wilson's later novels, especially his increasing use of symbolism; certainly *The Old Men at the Zoo* depends far more upon symbolism for its effect than any of his earlier works. Fable, as Golding employs it in *Lord of the Flies*, is another possible way of incorporating a sense of evil, but this approach Wilson rejects as not quite suitable for the traditional purposes of the novel.

Whatever the case with evil and the novel, it is clear that Wilson throughout his work has brought back to modern fiction some of the broad social setting (not "social significance" only, which is another thing) that we usually associate with the great nineteenth-century writers. He has freely and frequently acknowledged his debt to Dickens, whose minor characters are the direct ancestors of many of his own, such as Alice Cressett, Old Barker, Bill Pendlebury, and Dr Charles Langley-Beard. By rejecting the extremes of the early twentieth-century experimental novel, he shows himself in reaction to Bloomsbury aestheticism, but the humanism of Bloomsbury writers he has not entirely thrown over. On the contrary, he tries to fuse their more intellectually understood views with the wider vision of Dickens and the deeper sympathy of Dostoevsky. The combination leads to results that are a function of both Wilson's personality and his art. In his early stories and novels, one of the chief characteristics is his wit, which won for him immediate acclaim among the critics—and for whose return in greater abundance we still hear an occasional nostalgic plea. The wit is best described as Augustan, depending as it does upon a sharp but subtle incongruity of manner and matter, intention and event, conflicting emotional tones, and so forth. *Hemlock and After* provides many examples: "They parted with mutual respect and an even greater misunderstanding of one another"; "Sweat mingled with Mrs. Craddock's joyful tears"; "Mrs. Curry whispered loudly to Ron [of Bernard during his Vardon Hall speech], 'What a loving, passionate man he is!' "[2] This Augustan quality is comparable to Jane Austen's, another of Wilson's favourite authors who, seen along with the influence of Dickens and Dostoevsky, gives added testimony to Wilson's complex, almost contradictory nature as a writer and a person. At the end of *Pride and Prejudice*, Jane Austen says: "Miss Bingley's congratulations to her brother, on his approaching marriage, were all that was affectionate and insincere." As the passage continues, however, we see implications that go much further than purely verbal wit:

> She wrote even to Jane on the occasion, to express her delight, and repeat all her former professions of regard. Jane was not deceived, but she was affected; and though feeling no reliance on her, could not help writing her a much kinder answer than she knew she deserved.

The balanced statement of affection tempered by insight, the important qualifications of Jane Bennet's mature attitude to her prospective sister-in-law, so carefully conveyed by the rhetoric, suggest the sorts of awareness that characterise Wilson's work as well. This awareness looks forward, in his work as in Jane Austen's, to the later novels, where more profound juxtapositions of character and situation, and of ideas, eventually assume much greater importance for both writers.

In *Hemlock and After* and in the later novels, the juxta-position of character and situation that most interests Wilson is that in which the hero is suddenly confronted with a new and disturbing image of himself. Simon Carter in *The Old Men at the Zoo* differs from the others chiefly because he fails to recognise this development in his character, thus becoming an excellent target for satire, a villain almost, instead of a serious comic hero like Gerald Middleton or Meg Eliot. This image of the individual struggling against all kinds of hostile forces, including his own self-deceptions and lusts, in order to find some useful, dignified role for himself that still gives him pleasure is the heart of Wilson's humanism. Evil is whatever is life-destroying—emotionally, intellectually, or socially annihilating. Hence parasites like Mrs Curry and Sherman Winter or even Meg Eliot before her husband's death are embodiments of evil. But in trying to work out solutions for his characters, Wilson resists such "cosy" concepts of love and sweetness and coterie warmth that he finds objectionable, for example, in some of the novels of Christopher Isherwood.[3] Not only love, but sometimes hate, too, must be felt by an indi-vidual who is yet a human being. The problem of evil is not that people may hate each other, but that hate may gain complete control over a person, destroying his own humanity even as it tries to destroy others'.

In his criticism of another great writer and humanist, Albert Camus, Wilson's position becomes still clearer. He is principally concerned with the split in Camus' work that divorces his affirmation of life from any fully realised human being in his novels. This Wilson attributes to Camus' "personal convictions about life, convictions springing from a temperament that found elation in the presence of nature and depression in the contemplation of human behaviour."[4] But his response to Nature compelled him, with characteristic Gallic logic, to seek some comparable human affirmation. This logical discipline accounts for the rigour of his style, which accordingly manifests his honour as an artist. At the same time, it tends to crush the life out of his fiction, turning his characters into abstractions rather than men. For Wilson, this endangers Camus' position not only as a novelist, but as a humanist, too. The "love of mankind" is an inadequate humanism, he argues: "only an intensity of feeling—love mixed with hatred—for individual men and women" can protect a humanist from the abstract, "from drawing men and women according to his own hopes and fears."[5] No matter how defective (because too anarchic) this conception of humanism may appear to others, certainly Wilson has been faithful to it himself; it accounts for both the solid feel of his fiction and the personal engagement of his criticism.

C. B. Cox, in an intensive analysis of *Hemlock and After*, explores the further implications of this humanism. As we have suggested, for Wilson the first step for the modern humanist is "a proper recognition of the power of evil."[6] Since every human activity appears to partake of some measure of evil, the problem is then to limit the field of destruction, including self-destruction. Despair of human perfectibility, or at any rate despair over lost innocence and the pervasiveness of evil, may lead to the a-morally conceived but really vicious life of Hubert Rose, or it may follow Bernard and Ella's alternative of human compassion. From such compassion for others some sense of commitment may be born which, though it does not save Bernard, saves his wife. In the later novels, as we have seen, it saves Gerald and (more clearly and directly) Meg. In so far as compassion may degenerate into sentimentalism, however, it can ruin the lives of other characters, such as David Parker, unless they are warned. This is the warning that Terence Lambert issues to Elizabeth Sands, just as after him Dollie Stokesay, Meg Eliot, and Martha Carter caution their respective counterparts. So long as one resists the pitfalls of self-deception and its complement, cynicism; so long as one prepares for a world that is neither sweet nor cosy but still endurable and even, at times, pleasurable; to this extent one is truly equipped to meet life on its own terms, without recourse to the supra-human values of religion (a sentimental evasion in Wilson's view), or to the dehumanising values of science and the paternalism of bureaucracy.

Of all the manifestations of evil abroad in Britain to-day, Wilson most deplores those which he groups under "snobbery, intellectual dishonesty, and the so-called realistic cult of the expedient."[7] At the same time, he clearly recognises the struggle against flagrant social indecency, the amount of goodwill, and the gentleness that also characterise his countrymen; in fact, the striking absence of aggression among Englishmen, he says, has been a basic assumption of his fiction.[8] His humanism may be unsystematic—indeed, he eschews and even castigates dogma in these matters—for his primary concern is constantly with the individual, though he hardly endorses the "rugged individualism" of a former age. He is well aware of the abuses that this attitude has caused. Quite the contrary, he is leftist in his political and social thinking, if by "leftist" we can still imply a socialism that tries to keep men off soup queues without going on to meddle in their private lives. This dilemma suggests the central problem of Britain under the Opportunity State, as Wilson sees it; that is, how to steer the right course between reactionary individualism on the one hand, and welfare orthodoxy on the other.[9] He has no programme to offer, but the extent to which he is ready to protect the rights of the individual may be measured by his recent *avant-garde* attack upon almost all censorship of pornography. However sad or pathetic pornography addicts may be, he argues, "it is often by defending the little grubby freedoms of lonely men and women that we can justly demand greater, more important freedoms."[10]

In the meanwhile, Wilson continues to experiment with the traditional forms of his art. He realises that a writer who is content merely to repeat the successes of his earlier work is doomed, is dead. Television drama seems especially to hold out promise for him. His third television play, "The Invasion," couples his maturing gifts as a dramatist with a revived interest in science fiction, revived, apparently, by such books as Kingsley Amis's *New Maps of Hell*.[11] But in each of his roles as novelist, playwright, literary critic, and now university don—for he has recently accepted appointment to the new University of East Anglia—we can be certain that he will continue to exercise a stringent but healthful influence upon English life and letters. Focusing as he does upon the here-and-now, the mesh of local customs and concerns, he manages at the same time to keep in view the central problems of human existence that these ephemera so often tend to obscure. Like the great writers in whose tradition he has tried to follow, and from whose achievement he derives so much of his strength, Wilson constantly attempts in all of his work to uncover the real nature of our humanity. If in the process he has so far found little to inspire unrestrained rejoicing, nevertheless he has found no occasion to seek recourse in despair. As one of the most searching and articulate intellectuals in Britain to-day, he commands our most careful attention and respect.

REFERENCES

1. "Evil and the English Novel," 1963, p. 116.
2. *H.A.*, pp. 196, 127, 152.
3. "The New and the Old Isherwood," 1954, pp. 62–68.
4. "Albert Camus, Humanist," 1960, p. 293.
5. *Ibid.*
6. "The Humanism of Angus Wilson: A Study of *Hemlock and After*," 1961, p. 234.
7. "Fourteen Points," 1962, p. 11.
8. "This Gentl'd Isle," 1955, p. 85.
9. "A Critic in Utopia," 1961, p. 25.
10. "Not for Banning," 1962, pp. 50–51.
11. See "The Status of S.F.," 1961, p. 28.

BIBLIOGRAPHY

I. ANGUS WILSON

1. Stories and Novels

The Wrong Set and Other Stories. London (Secker & Warburg) 1949.
Such Darling Dodos and Other Stories. London (Secker & Warburg) 1950.
Hemlock and After. London (Secker & Warburg) 1952.
Anglo-Saxon Attitudes. London (Secker & Warburg) 1956.
A Bit Off the Map and Other Stories. London (Secker & Warburg) 1957.
The Middle Age of Mrs Eliot. London (Secker & Warburg) 1958.
The Old Men at the Zoo. London (Secker & Warburg) 1961.
"My Husband Is Right," in *Texas Quarterly*, IV (Autumn 1961) pp. 139–45.

2. Plays and Radio Plays

The Mulberry Bush. London (Secker & Warburg) 1956.
"Skeletons and Assegais," in *Transatlantic Review*, 9 (Spring 1962) pp. 19–43.

3. Miscellaneous

Émile Zola: An Introductory Study of his Novels. London (Secker & Warburg) 1952.
For Whom the Cloche Tolls: A Scrap-Book of the Twenties (with Philippe Jullian). London (Methuen) 1953.
"Envy," in *The Seven Deadly Sins*, intro. by Raymond Mortimer. (Sunday Times Publications Ltd.) 1962.
The Wild Garden. Berkeley (University of California Press) and London (Secker & Warburg) 1963.

4. Selected Essays and Criticism

"Letter from London," in *American Mercury*, LXXII (May 1951), pp. 571–7.
"Revolution in British Reading," in *American Mercury*, LXXIII (Dec. 1951), pp. 47–54.
"Throughout the Country," in *New Statesman*, XLV (13 Jun. 1953), pp. 696 ff.
"The New and the Old Isherwood" [review of Christopher Isherwood, *The World in the Evening*], in *Encounter*, Aug. 1954, pp. 62–8.

"The Short Story Changes," in the *Spectator*, cxcviii (1 Oct. 1954), p. 402.

"The Naive Emancipator" [review of Aldous Huxley, *The Genius and the Goddess*], in *Encounter*, Jul. 1955, pp. 73–6.

"To Know and Yet Not to Fear Reality" [review of Lionel Trilling, *The Opposing Self*], in *Encounter*, Aug. 1955, pp. 79–82.

"This Gentl'd Isle" [review of Geoffrey Gorer, *Exploring British Character*], in *Encounter*, Sep. 1955, pp. 84–7.

"The World's Greatest Museum," in *Holiday*, xviii (Sep. 1955), pp. 48 ff.

"The Heart of Lawrence" [review of F. R. Leavis, *D. H. Lawrence*], in *Encounter*, Dec. 1955, pp. 81–3.

"Exorcising the Past" [review of A. L. Rowse, *The Expansion of Elizabethan England*], in *Encounter*, Jan. 1956, pp. 86–8.

"Galsworthy's Forsyte Saga," in *New Statesman*, li (3 Mar. 1956), p. 187.

"Novels and Highbrows" [review of George H. Ford, *Dickens and his Readers*], in *Encounter*, Apr. 1956, pp. 75–7.

"A.D. 1956" [review of Arnold Toynbee, *An Historian's Approach to Religion*], in *Encounter*, Oct. 1956, pp. 80–3.

"New Novels" [review of novels by William Cooper, Irwin Shaw, and others], in *Encounter*, Aug. 1956, pp. 83–6.

"Suicides in London" [review of Peter Sainsbury, *Suicide in London*], in *Encounter*, Dec. 1956, pp. 83–5.

"A Church of Compromise" [review of G. K. Balleine, *Past Finding Out*], in *Encounter*, Feb. 1957, pp. 81–3.

"A Century of Japanese Writing" [review of *Modern Japanese Literature*, ed. Donald Keene], in *Encounter*, Apr. 1957, pp. 83–5.

"Revolt of Samuel Butler," in *Atlantic Monthly*, cc (Nov. 1957), pp. 190–8.

"A Conversation with E. M. Forster," in *Encounter*, Nov. 1957, pp. 52–7.

"Bexhill and After," in the *Spectator*, ccii (9 May 1958), pp. 583–4.

"The Jolliest Resort in the World," in *Holiday*, xxiv (Aug. 1958), pp. 46 ff.

"Diversity and Depth," in *The Times Literary Supplement*, lvii (15 Aug. 1958), p. viii.

"The Literary View" [review of William Cooper, *Prince Genji*], in the *Observer*, 8 Feb. 1959, p. 19.

"Realist or Romantic?" [review of H. J. Hunt, *Balzac's Comedie Humaine*], in the *Observer*, 26 Apr. 1959, p. 23.

"The Intellectual on the Aisle" [review of Mary McCarthy, *Sights and Spectacles*], in *Encounter*, Jun. 1959, pp. 68–70.

"Man of Letters" [review of Christopher Hassall, *Edward Marsh*], in the *Spectator*, cciii (12 Jun. 1959), p. 861.

"New Playwrights" [review of new plays by Shelagh Delaney, Doris Lessing, Bernard Kops, and Arnold Wesker], in *Partisan Review*, XXVI (Fall 1959), pp. 631–4.

"Fulfillment in Time" [review of G. D. Painter, *Marcel Proust: A Biography*], in the *Observer*, 20 Sep. 1959, p. 22.

"Room at the Top-ism," in the *Spectator*, CCIII (2 Oct. 1959), p. 435.

"Rescuing the Workers" [review of Clancy Sigall, *Weekend in Dinlock*], in the *Spectator*, CCIV (29 Jan. 1960), pp. 140–1.

"Albert Camus, Humanist," in the *Spectator*, CCIV (26 Feb. 1960), pp. 293–4.

"Going to Ground" [review of Raleigh Trevelyan, *A Hermit Disclosed*], in the *Observer*, 13 Mar. 1960, p. 20.

"Charles Dickens: A Haunting," in the *Critical Quarterly*, II (Summer 1960), pp. 101–8.

"Pictures of Health" [review of Richard Rees, *For Love or Money*], in the *Observer*, 14 Aug. 1960, p. 20.

"The Status of S. F." [review of Kingsley Amis, *New Maps of Hell*], in the *Observer*, 12 Mar. 1961, p. 28.

"A Critic in Utopia" [review of Kathleen Nott, *A Clean, Well-Lighted Place*], in the *Observer*, 25 Jan. 1961, p. 25.

"The Whites in South Africa," in *Partisan Review*, XXVIII (1961), pp. 612–32.

"The Heroes and Heroines of Dickens," in *Review of English Literature*, II (Jul. 1961) pp. 7–18.

"Outsider on Olympus" [review of A. O. J. Cockshut, *The Imagination of Charles Dickens*], in the *Observer*, 22 Aug. 1961, p. 18.

"Fourteen Points," in *Encounter*, Jan. 1962, pp. 10–12.

"South African Exiles" [review of Patrick van Rensburg, *Guilty Land* and Myra Blumberg, *White Madam*], in the *Observer*, 21 Jan. 1962, p. 31.

"Not for Banning" [review of *To Deprave and Corrupt*, ed. John Chandos], in *New Statesman*, LXIV (13 Jul. 1962), pp. 50–1.

"Social Reform and Mr Scrooge" [review of Philip Collins, *Dickens and Crime*], in the *Observer*, 5 Aug. 1962, p. 14.

"The Theatre of Three or Four" [review of John Bowen, *The Essay Prize*], in *The Listener*, LXVIII (30 Aug. 1962), p. 327.

"The Tragic View of Life" [review of John Wain, *Sprightly Running*], in the *Observer*, 16 Sep. 1962, p. 22.

"Evil in the English Novel" [based on the Northcliffe Lectures, 1961], in *The Listener*, LXVIII (27 Dec. 1962), pp. 1079–80, LXIX (3 Jan. 1963), pp. 15–16, LXIX (10 Jan. 1963), pp. 63–5, LXIX (17 Jan. 1963), pp. 115–17.

"Mythology in John Cowper Powys's Novels," in *Review of English Literature*, IV (Jan. 1963), pp. 9–20.

II. OTHERS

COCKSHUT, A. O. J.: "Favored Sons: The Moral World of Angus Wilson," in *Essays in Criticism*, IX (1959), pp. 50–60.

COX, C. B.: "The Humanism of Angus Wilson: A Study of *Hemlock and After*," in *Critical Quarterly*, III (1961), pp. 227–37.

GINDIN, JAMES: "Angus Wilson's Qualified Nationalism," in *Postwar British Fiction*. Berkeley 1962.

JENKINS, A.: "Hemlock—and Before," in the *Spectator*, CXCIII (17 Sep. 1954), p. 331.

ROSSELLI, J.: "Miss Schlegel, Meet Mr. Angus Wilson," in *New Statesman*, XLV (14 Mar. 1953), pp. 290 f.

SCOTT-KILVERT, IAN: "Angus Wilson," in *Review of English Literature*, I (1960), pp. 42–53.

WAIN, JOHN: "Comment on Widowhood," in the *New Yorker*, 11 Apr. 1959, pp. 164 ff.

Writers at Work: The Paris Review Interviews, ed. Malcolm Cowley. London 1959.